Relax, You're Already Home

RAYMOND BARNETT, PH.D.

Relax, You're Already Home

*Everyday Taoist Habits
for a Richer Life*

JEREMY P. TARCHER/PENGUIN

A MEMBER OF PENGUIN GROUP (USA) INC.   NEW YORK

JEREMY P. TARCHER/PENGUIN
Published by the Penguin Group
www.penguin.com

Penguin Group (USA) Inc., 375 Hudson Street, New York, New York 10014, USA •
Penguin Group (Canada), 10 Alcorn Avenue, Toronto, Ontario, Canada M4V 3B2 (a division
of Pearson Penguin Canada Inc.) • Penguin Books Ltd, 80 Strand, London WC2R 0RL, England •
Penguin Ireland, 25 St Stephen's Green, Dublin 2, Ireland (a division of Penguin
Books Ltd) • Penguin Group (Australia), 250 Camberwell Road, Camberwell, Victoria 3124, Australia
(a division of Pearson Australia Group Pty Ltd) • Penguin Books India
Pvt Ltd, 11 Community Centre, Panchsheel Park, New Delhi—110 017, India. • Penguin Group (NZ),
Cnr Airborne and Rosedale Roads, Albany, Auckland 1310, New Zealand (a division of Pearson
New Zealand Ltd) • Penguin Books (South Africa) (Pty) Ltd, 24 Sturdee Avenue,
Rosebank, Johannesburg 2196, South Africa

Penguin Books Ltd, Registered Offices: 80 Strand, London WC2R 0RL, England

Chinese characters drawn by Aiping Zhang, Chico, CA. Photograph of John Muir courtesy
of Radanovich Photography, Mariposa, CA. All other photos by the author.
Blondie comic strips used with permission of Reed Brennan Media Associates, Orlando, FL.
Newspaper article in Appendix 1 reprinted with permission of *St. Petersburg Times*, St. Petersburg, FL.

Most Tarcher/Penguin books are available at special quantity discounts for bulk purchase for sales
promotions, premiums, fund-raising, and educational needs. Special books or book excerpts also can be
created to fit specific needs. For details, write Penguin Group (USA) Inc. Special Markets, 375
Hudson Street, New York, NY 10014.

Library of Congress Cataloging-in-Publication Data

Barnett, Raymond.
Relax, you're already home: everyday Taoist habits for a richer life / by Raymond Barnett.
p.   cm.
ISBN 1-58542-366-1
1. Conduct of life.   2. Taoism—Miscellanea.   I. Title.

BJ1595.B33   2005   2004055373
99.5'1444—dc22

Printed in the United States of America
1   3   5   7   9   10   8   6   4   2

This book is printed on acid-free paper. ♾

BOOK DESIGN BY KATE NICHOLS

Acknowledgments

I would like to thank my neighbors in Valley Oaks Village for permission to use vignettes of our common life in "the village." I profited from Dr. John Nelson's thoughts and material on Taoism and Shintoism. Taoist Master Liu Ming was an early and inspiring guide into the world of Taoism. Calligraphy was kindly provided by Dr. Aiping Zhang and Dr. Weikun Cheng. Linyi Maslin's instruction in t'ai chi ch'uan three decades ago has seeped into many areas of my life. Detailed and myriad lessons in "the art of living" were kindly provided by my daughters Heather and Holly and their mother, Donna, and my son and daughter, Louis and Ashlyn, and their mother, Tammy. I have been blessed to have such traveling companions as Kyle Brown and A. J. Dickinson, who have shared many adventures and cold rainy nights. The manuscript benefited from the sharp eyes of my editor, Terri Hennessy, and the skill of Tarcher/Penguin's graphics team. And finally: thanks to the rocks, plants, animals, and especially waters of Bidwell Park here in Chico, the source of endless solace, wonder, and good times for my family and me.

Note on Romanization

I generally use the traditional Wade-Giles system of romanization for Chinese terms, since it is the one most familiar to people. For common terms which may be frequently encountered elsewhere, the modern pinyin romanization is also noted.

To Tam, Ash & Lou—

beloved fellow-travelers

along The Way

Contents

Prologue

What do you think: can the world's oldest continuous civilization have anything to say to the world's youngest?

China's culture—its everyday habits of life and the values they embody—is more than five thousand years old. America's is less than five hundred.

You can do the math.

The Chinese "way of life" wears well. Because it works so well, it retains its characteristic stamp wherever it's transplanted around the world. Molded by the ancient native outlook of Taoism, China's people practice a way of living their everyday life that is robust, cohesive, and above all successful. It is the flourishing constant underlying the changing superstructures of empire, republic, warlords, and now communism.

Can we in America learn anything from this old and fabulously successful way of living life?

Do we have any need for a different approach to life?

In my home state of California, there are more people in prison than in college. The state legislature and our governor regularly transform problems into crises, with the cost passed straight on to citizens like you and me. Big business and big labor alike buy special consideration. Money talks, and how.

On the national scene, you can't help but notice that the spasm of unity following 9/11 is long gone, and we're as bitterly divided as ever over war and peace, racism, the economy versus the environment, and how we should raise and educate our kids.

All this confusion and strife isn't confined to the public sphere, unfortunately. It's amply reflected in our private lives. Whether our jobs and relationships are steady or constantly changing, we all ask the same questions, just below the surface of our busy lives. What's this all about? Am I really happy, or just too busy to confront the fact that my life doesn't have a direction, a purpose?

Religion is supposed to answer these questions, of course. But some of us see traditional religions as hopelessly out of touch with the modern, scientific understanding of life. We wander into "New Age" ways of thinking. Others reach back to earlier and simpler versions of religion, fueling the contemporary resurgence in fundamentalist branches of Christianity and Islam. And those of us sticking with the religion we were raised in feel too often like we're just going through the motions, and we wonder, deep down, if the old explanations really work for us.

Why don't we try thinking *really* outside the box? Something really weird—but successful! Of course, from our American point of view, that's China. Those five thousand years of a culture that works so well that it really hasn't changed fundamentally for millennia. A culture that works so well that when its people move to Karachi or London or San Francisco, they take it with them, lock, stock, and barrel, giving the world all those Chinatowns in every corner of the planet.

On my first trips to Asia—Vietnam in the late 60s, courtesy of Uncle Sam, then China several times in the early 80s with my travel buddy Kyle—I immediately noticed how strange these places were, and how the daily lives of the people there had a different "flavor" than I'd ever seen. Since I'd studied the Chinese language while at Yale, and because Kyle is adventuresome and cool-witted, we were able to connect with the people way beyond the typical tourist level. The "different way of living" in China and the surrounding countries fascinated me, and I sought out the common people in little-traveled corners of China and Korea and Taiwan and Japan in subsequent trips.

Everywhere I found people exhibiting a tough acceptance of life, an ability to plunge into both the sweet and the bitter sides of life and savor it. I was struck by a simple, easygoing enjoyment of everyday life evident in many people, a low-key gusto that was at odds with life in much of America. The trite "serenity" that you hear so much about turned out to be true, and not among gurus and hermits, but among many of the common folk I encountered.

Between my travels and my study, it became apparent that the ancient Taoist approach to life accounted for much of what I was seeing. Not the Taoism of the advanced Masters, with their dramatic feats of martial arts and exotic breathing techniques, but the *Taoism of the common people, the real China.* Long described in China as "the art of living," Taoism is the oldest continuous and consistent approach to living on the planet. This Taoist outlook is thoroughly ingrained in everyday life in China, so that daily life is permeated by Taoist habits. The accumulation of these simple Taoist habits, it turns out, gives rise to that richer, more vibrant, steadily focused quality of life that I saw throughout China.

You can tap into that richer life. Right here in America, today. And you don't have to "go Chinese" and start meditating and practicing vicious high-leg kicks to do it. *All you need to do is incorporate the simple, everyday Taoist habits into your existing life.* I'll get you started in the following pages, and give you lots of suggestions about what has worked for me, my family, and many others. Let's go!

CHAPTER 1

Immersion in the Tao

The Taoist tradition has given rise to countless everyday habits of the ordinary people of China, habits which contribute to a rich, coherent experience of life. These everyday Taoist habits work just as well for Americans as for Chinese, though. In fact, you and I practice many of them, unaware of what's behind them.

Take the view of things I have from my kitchen window here in northern California, for example. As I stare out the window filling the teapot with water first thing every morning, I usually see Julie from across the way coming back from her dawn run. She's beaming, cheeks flushed, walking with a lilt. And most evenings, while doing the dinner dishes in the same spot, I see Jay from the other end of our CoHousing community, arriving home from a brisk stroll in the park with my neighbors George and Judy. They're laughing, and there's a comfortable swagger in their steps.

We've all witnessed these scenes. Maybe you're the one doing the jogging or the walking. Why do these particular activities make us feel so good? Why do folks carve time out of their busy days to walk, to jog, to visit a park?

The same sort of scenes occur in China, although the details are different. When my buddy Kyle and I first traveled independently in China in 1986, we'd rise before dawn and walk to the nearest park. There, we'd see crowds of people doing the graceful, sweeping moves of t'ai chi ch'uan, or the violent lunges of kung fu with swords and lances. Some older folks were simply walking deliberately along a course, hands making circular movements in the chill air.

When you survey Chinese art over the ages, you notice how many paintings there are of lone individuals or small groups of friends in the mountains, or in a bamboo grove, or, very frequently, beside a stream. Usually these folks are playing a friendly board game, or drinking tea, or often just sitting quietly, enjoying the scenery.

What's going on in these traditional activities? Are the Chinese participating in the same sort of experience as the neighbors outside my kitchen window? In China, at least, people do these outdoor activities because the Taoist outlook permeating Chinese culture places a huge premium on humans connecting with the forces inherent in the natural world. This keeps people healthy and happy. Preeminent among these forces that structure and permeate the natural world is the Tao. *These folks are connecting with the Tao.*

Tao (the way, or path, pronounced "dow" and spelled "Dao" in the pinyin system) confers the inherent nature of each material and force in the universe. Tao is the backdrop and the impetus for everything that happens, all the myriad processes of transformation that constantly course through the world. In the words of a Japanese scholar, Tao is "the mood of the universe." The flow of Tao gives rise to the patterns and regularities that characterize the universe. Tao courses everywhere, but most clearly in the natural world, where its patterns are strikingly evident, most accessible to human perception and participation.

So we humans connect with this most elemental of phenomena by spending time in the natural world, by participating in the flow of life in nature. Activity in nature reminds us of "the way things are," realigns us with the mood of the universe, the bedrock of existence—of our own existence, as well as everything else.

Paramount among Taoist habits for us modern Americans, then, is doing in our society what those Chinese have been doing in theirs for

Tao

- *Path, Way*
- *Pattern*
- *Transformation*
- *"Mood" of universe*
- *The way things are*

thousands of years: spend time in the natural world. **Immersing ourselves in the Tao is the most basic Taoist habit**. This is so important to our health, both physical and spiritual, that it should be done every day.

How do we daily immerse ourselves in the Tao in the modern West? Renouncing your job and family and moving to a shack in the woods is not required. (Although some do: see Appendix 1, about NASCAR driver Ward Burton.) Do you have a park or green space reasonably close to your home? Go there, every day if you can. Make it a routine part of your day. If you're a morning person, then early morning is prime. Julie across the way from me knows this. Although she has two energetic youngsters, she manages to be up early every day for her jog through the park, before her husband, Richard, leaves for his work. We all know the air is fresher, the day more charged with positive potential just after dawn. Prime time to be out in the natural world.

If you're not a morning person, then visit the park on your lunch hour, or first thing after school or work. This is Jay's, George's, and Judy's walk schedule. In general, engaging in some movement among the trees and rocks is best—walking, bicycling, jogging. But just sitting in the natural environment is beneficial, especially near a body of water. Creeks are magnets for Taoists.

We are fortunate here to live just a block from the third largest municipal park in America. All day long, my neighbors stream out of Valley Oaks Village, our CoHousing com-

Water shows the shape and flow of Tao.

munity. On foot, bicycles, or skates, we head for Bidwell Park. You cannot spend five minutes in our section of the park without encountering a neighbor. We have our favorite corners, our favorite swimming holes in the park's Chico Creek, our favorite paths and trees and rocks.

You're not close to a park? Or you're not particularly athletic? If you have a bit of dirt around your home, start a garden, either flower or vegetable. Tend it, as much of the year as your climate permits. Mulch it, fertilize it, take deep breaths as you work the soil, drawing into your lungs the delicious dirt smell produced by the millions of *Streptomyces* bacteria residing there. Start a compost pile if your neighbors will stand it, and recycle your food and lawn wastes. Tending your garden puts you in touch with the flow of the Tao, focuses you on the natural rhythms of the universe.

No park or dirt nearby? Bring the natural world into your home. Invest in a variety of house plants, and care for them. Learn which of your windows the plants are happiest beside. Which water regimes they thrive on. Which nutrients keep them healthy and luxuriant. Do they need "grow lights" in the winter to stay happy? The Tao flows in electrical appliances also!

Immersion in the Tao

How many of these can you do today? This week?

> *Walk or jog in a park;*
> > *notice the trees and rocks.*
> *Eat lunch outdoors;*
> > *note clouds and breezes.*
> *Sit beside a lake, creek, or the ocean;*
> > *wade in and explore its rocks and creatures.*
> *Bicycle in the countryside;*
> > *take a picnic, pick some flowers.*
> *Start a small garden;*
> > *feel the dirt, make it richer.*

Exploring Your Terrain

Visit every park or green space in your town over the next week or month. Describe each one, and the possibilities each one offers for immersion in the Tao.

Visit every body of water in your county over the next month or year. Describe each one, and the possibilities each one offers for immersion in the Tao.

Learn to identify five native trees in your county. Describe their leaf shape, what type of fruit they produce, what birds and insects and mammals you find in them.

Buy binoculars and learn ten common birds in your area. What vegetation do they hang out in? What do they eat? What do their calls sound like?

What natural object intrigues you when you go for a trip or a walk? Pick it up, bring it home, and put it on your windowsill. In our home we have lots of rocks and seashells on shelves and counters as well as windowsills. Not just any rocks or seashells, but special ones, rocks spewed from volcanoes in Hawaii, or seashells formed by mollusks that have poison darts to subdue their wormy or fishy prey. Just seeing the rocks and shells there reminds you of how incredible the world is, and how much fun you had when you found them.

The practice of immersing yourself in the Tao applies to very mundane aspects of your daily life. When I had just graduated from high school, I had a summer job working construction in Tulsa. I rode to work with Dad at 6:45 every morning. Dad had every window in the car down, and since I was wearing a T-shirt appropriate for the hottest part of the day, I was freezing in the early-morning coolness. I didn't say anything—this was the very early 1960s in Oklahoma, and you didn't dare say much to your dad, certainly not request him to change his habits. Dad's instinct was to have as much fresh air as possible around him. He had grown up on a farm in central Oklahoma, and being outdoors in nature was just second nature to him, even though he'd traded his tractor for the executive suite of a petroleum-supply firm.

Like my dad, open your windows as much as possible. Don't hide inside your closed home with a heater or air conditioner any more than you have to. In the summers, we turn the AC off at night, open our windows, and let the universe cool the house down.

Do you ever go camping? Incorporate camping trips into your family life. Every summer, a time or two, my wife, Tammy, and I drive two hours north to Lassen Park with our kids Ash and Lou, and pitch our tent for a long weekend. We've always had a large family tent. It's just part of our essential family "tool kit," like first-aid kits, and bicycles, and apples always available on the kitchen table.

You don't think your family will take to camping? Make it fun. How many matches does Dad need to start the fire? Is he allowed to use newspapers as kindling? At what age do your kids get better at making the fire than Dad? Which trail are you hiking today? How many s'mores can my son Lou gorge himself on tonight?

We buy "light sticks," the plastic tubes containing substances that glow when you break the internal partition separating them, and take them camping with us. Every night we entertain ourselves for hours after settling into our bedrolls in the tent, swirling the glowing containers in different patterns on the end of a string, or bending the long, flexible ones into intriguing shapes. We make butterflies that flutter around the tent, or lumbering giant pandas. Then the kids nestle

---

Sit Down Today and Plan a
Camping Trip with Family or Friends

YOUR IDEAS

Possible sites within two hours: _____

Unusual food treat to bring: _____

For simple entertainment—lightsticks, and: _____

Fire-making ingredients: _____

Field guides for hikes, animals: _____

One comfort of home: _____

Something weird & zany: _____

Don't forget tent and rain gear!

beside the glowing sticks, their own personal lighted guardians through the chilly nights.

Why does time in natural environments benefit us, from a scientific view? That's easy to explain. Humans evolved for millions of years on the savannas of Africa. We moved out of Africa into the rest of the Old World, then to the New World, living completely immersed in nature. Sensory input from the natural world is part of our biological heritage, part of what has been incorporated into the normal functioning of our genes, our nervous systems, our guts. When we cut ourselves off from the natural world, our biological systems are adrift, missing key elements of the system of cues they are accustomed to receive. Sensory input from the natural world is so fundamental that, like fish in water, we don't even realize how critical it is. But just look at people living in crowded cities to realize how easily many of us get "off track" without it, feeling frazzled and off center, and wondering what's gone wrong.

Tiny frogs of the family Dendrobatidae inhabit rain forests in South America. These are the creatures which produce the deadly alkaloid poisons that Cocos Indians rub on their darts to bring down large prey. The alkaloids cause sodium and potassium channels in cell membranes to misfunction. When you capture a Dendrobatid frog and take it to a laboratory in a city, the poor creature ceases producing the poisons that protect it. Why? We can't figure it out. Thought it was the food. Nope. There's something about just living in that rain-forest environment that turns on the frog's "poison" genes to express themselves. Perhaps the sounds. Perhaps the smells. Perhaps the whole experience of living in the natural world where it evolved. Remove it from those inputs, and it's missing something. It's "off center," things aren't "right."

You and I are just like these frogs. And so are redwood trees and banana slugs. We all evolved in the natural world. We need it to stay healthy, to keep our systems functioning well. Take us out of the natural environment, isolate us from the natural world and its flow of Tao, and we suffer.

Immerse yourself in the Tao. It keeps you centered. Healthier. Happier. More resilient when tough times come. The Tao is the sacred stuff that animates the universe. Cleave to it.

Postscript for Families

If you're single or part of a couple without kids, immersing yourself in the Tao every day is not too difficult. If you're a parent raising kids, it can be a tremendous challenge just to find the time and opportunity to get *yourself* in the natural world every day. Get your kids there every day, too? Forget it!

I hear you. But the more often you can manage to immerse your kids in the natural world, the healthier they'll be, too. Don't be a dictator about it, but do what you can to get those kids away from the television or computer and outside with you. I know it's not easy. Ash and Lou, my two youngest kids, get "stuck" in front of their computer and favorite videos,

Find Your "Laughin' Place"

Among Heather's and Holly's favorite stories when they were young were the Brer Rabbit stories. They especially liked the one about Brer Rabbit's escape from Brer Fox at his "Laughin' Place," an old hickory tree full, as it turned out, of bumblebees.

Devote this weekend to finding your own Laughin' Place, an outdoors spot that just makes you feel good to be there. A spot that makes you feel connected. A spot where the particular configuration of the Tao fits with your nature, and makes you want to laugh in delight.

You may find your Laughin' Place at one of the parks in your town. Or you may want to drive out to the countryside or up to the mountains or to the seashore to find it. But you'll know it when you find it. There'll be a "rightness" to its look and feel. A sigh of contentment will bubble out of you as you see it and hear it. Drag a lawn chair out, or buckle into your snowboard, and enjoy it. Visit it often! It's your Laughin' Place.

like most modern kids. Tammy and I put limits on the amount of "electronic monitor" time the kids can do every day. We prohibit any television at all, which admittedly might be tough for many families, although if you establish the pattern from the get-go, it is surprisingly doable. But still, it's sometimes tough to get the kids off their duffs and into the park

"Gator Junior," a Barnett Family Laughin' Place

with us. It usually helps to get a couple of their buddies to come along. Without fail, the kids love it once they get there.

When you're in the natural environment with your kids, play some games. Joseph Cornell's *Sharing Nature with Children* books (1979 and 1989) are fabulous sources of fun things to do with kids in nature. Cornell's activities go beyond "fun" to incorporate an appreciation for the spiritual and other values of activity in the natural world. These books can be thought of as manuals for Taoist living for families.

CHAPTER 2

Realizing You're Already Home

Do you sometimes feel a little lost? Like you're not sure about what it means to be an adult? Maybe like you're a little kid still, deep inside, and just pretending to be an adult, hoping people don't notice that you're making things up as you go? Do you sometimes wonder where "home" is, that place where you feel right and secure and confident about yourself?

I felt this way most of my adult life, even while raising my two oldest daughters, Heather and Holly. *Especially* while raising Heather and Holly! I wondered if everyone felt this way, deep down. Then I began to travel to China, and on a mountain in the deepest corner of China I discovered how to get home, to a place that feels right.

Trailside pharmacy on
Mt. Emei

Kyle and I happened to hit Mt. Emei, deep in Szechuan next to Tibet, during the early spring monsoon. A.J. was with us, an old Yale friend I'd bumped into in Peking. The weather was miserable, for humans at least—great for slime molds and slugs, though. We were drenched to the bone, and cold.

Along the muddy pathway up Mt. Emei we encountered frequent little stalls selling hot tea, duck eggs, and a variety of very bizarre items: the dried hind foot of a monkey, snake-skins curled up in a tight spiral, mushrooms of every variety, bits of dried roots. The Chinese climb mountains because they're sacred, and climbing them brings you closer to Heaven and increases the flow of Ch'i energy through you. These bizarre items beside the trail are part of that endeavor: ground up and put into that hot tea in certain combinations, they help increase the flow of Ch'i in the pilgrim. The pilgrim becomes healthier, feels better on many levels. *Ch'i "works" in humans in exactly the same way it works in mushrooms and ducks and monkeys, because humans are part and parcel of the flow of energy and transformations in the world.* Or, as a modern Western scientist would say, the basic structure and chemical ingredients of human DNA and proteins and the biochemical transformations these molecules constantly undergo are the same in mushrooms and ducks and monkeys.

Ch'i (pronounced "chee," and spelled "Qi" in the pinyin system) can be translated as "energy," or "pulse," or "breath," or "wind." It's the agent that Tao utilizes in its pattern-giving aspect, the restless push through which Tao is manifested in the endless transformations of existence. Ch'i itself can be

Ch'i

• *Energy*
• *Breath*

grouped into its yin aspects (soft, yielding, earthly, feminine) and its yang aspects (hard, aggressive, heavenly, masculine). Taoism sees all things (*wan wu,* "the ten thousand things") as unique and characteristic combinations of yin and yang. "All things carry yin and embrace yang," says the *Tao Te Ching.* "They achieve harmony by combining these forces."

The same goes for humans. We humans are nothing extraordinary. Like redwoods and blue whales and granite and water, we have our own characteristic balance of yin and yang. We are no better or worse than anything else in the universe. *We are what we are,* just as banana slugs are what banana slugs are.

As Kyle, A.J., and I trudged through the cold rain up Mt. Emei, two Taoist truths began to stir in me, as I thought about the Ch'i in the dried snakeskins and the mushrooms. How it flows through humans as well as snakes and mushrooms. First, since the Tao inheres in us humans just as it inheres in redwoods, and since the Ch'i flows through us in our characteristic way, just as it flows through banana slugs in their characteristic way, it follows that we humans are in a fundamental sense "okay." **This is the first Taoist truth about humans: we are already what we are meant to be.** We are not broken, or dramatically lost, or in need of fixing or salvation. So powerful and fundamental are Tao and Ch'i that it is not possible for us to depart far from them. **Each of us is already "home"** in the deepest sense. We are what we are supposed to be, just as a blue whale is already what it is supposed to be.

Good news! Wonderful, exhilarating news. We are, in fact, okay. We are home, already home. The world is a marvelous place and we humans belong in it and are worthwhile, integral parts of that marvelous whole.

"Whoa!" you say. What about that deep-down feeling sometimes, that we're just faking things, that we're not, in fact,

Tao Works Through Ch'i

to Manifest the Ten Thousand Things

home? Where does that come from?! And what about those monkey bones and snakeskins along the trail up Mt. Emei? If we're already home, why are we worried about changing our Ch'i by ingesting all sorts of weird stuff?

Good questions. That brings us to **the second Taoist truth about humans: we are rather easily and regularly nudged a bit off course by our environment.** Each creature has its own combination of yin and yang. Banana slugs are different from redwoods. Humans are different from other creatures primarily in being more neurologically complex and sensitive. Scientists would say this is due to the hyperdevelopment of the human central nervous system and its attendant sensory receptors. Now, this heightened sensitivity gives us deep emotions and wonderful music and art. But it also means that we humans are strongly affected by the flow of Ch'i in our environment, both from other creatures (plants, other animals, including humans) and from things like sunsets and fields of wildflowers and violent movies and being drenched to the bone by cold rain on a mountain.

This heightened sensitivity to the flow of Ch'i in our environment results in our being easily and regularly nudged off course by our interactions with the world. Our personal, individual "setting" of the general human balance of yin and yang is always getting tipped away from our optimal balance. We get too yin, or too yang. Not by a lot. We couldn't depart very far from what we are. We are, in fact, already home in the most fundamental sense. But we certainly can and do get bumped out of optimal balance—the second Taoist truth about humans.

So we all occasionally feel a bit "lost," not on track the way we'd like to be. And if we misunderstand what's going on, if we miscalculate and panic about this feeling, we can really

Mt. Emei's Two Truths:

We're already "home" where we belong.
We're easily nudged a bit "off center."

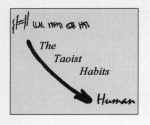

The
Taoist
Habits

Human

get bent out of shape. Frazzled, way off balance. Off center. Maybe even despairing.

Hence the mushrooms and roots and dried snakeskins along the trail up Mt. Emei. Hence the deer antlers and feng shui and acupuncture and t'ai chi you see so prominent throughout China. These are all mild methods to regularly nudge us back on track, to keep us from straying too far from home. Indeed, all the daily Taoist habits that permeate everyday life in China are similar mild methods to keep the people there on track.

What are the specific habits that we can adopt here in America to reflect these two Taoist truths about humans? The habits to nudge *us* back on track? A whole range of habits flow from these two truths, but they can, in general, be grouped into two overarching and very general habits.

The first Taoist habit emerging from these truths is that we can relax. We're already home. All we need is a bit of fine-tuning to unclutter the view. Relaxing encompasses both our *attitude* and our *actions*. We can drop our attitude of fear and panic. There's no need to rush around pursuing dramatic projects to fundamentally improve ourselves. No need to enroll in crash courses to "fix" broken hearts or minds or bodies. No heroics are called for. In fact, heroic measures only succeed in pushing us farther away from who we really are, and almost always fail to stick in the long run. Dramatic conversions and life changes make great TV and bring money to evangelists and gurus alike, but they don't last long, typically. They are fantasies, and fantasies take extraordinary amounts of energy to sustain. And often money as well.

We're constantly being told by very powerful, sophisticated, and intrusive media that we're in trouble. That we're dangerously far from whole. That we need to quickly purchase some "things" to fix a serious problem, whether it's mouthwash or cool basketball shoes or a seminar in "self-actualization" or a home with a three-car garage in a gated community. So we take half a dozen quick breaths, clench our teeth, reach for the checkbook, and plunge into a frantic endeavor to solve our "problem," to fix what's so horribly "broken" about us.

Relax. Relax into who you really are. Nothing is required to get home. It's right here; no need to search across forbidding landscapes to get there. *Your home is right in the center of you. Not far!* The farther afield you roam in search of yourself, the farther away from your center you wander. It's possible to get really confused and feel thoroughly lost if you bend considerable energy to fighting your way past threatening obstacles, to fleeing away from your center. The good news, though, is that it's possible to find your way back. All you need to do is relax, abandon the feverish pursuit, and come home to the center you carry within you. Attend to the Tao that inheres in every cell of you. Let the Ch'i flow simply and purely through you. Welcome home.

Remembering You're Home, and Enjoying Life

Buy a nice journal today, a durable one, with a look you like. In the following weeks and months, write in it the activities that make you happy, the times that bring a smile to your face, the things you've done that make your heart feel full.

When you're feeling low and bent out of shape, pick up the journal and read through it. Remind yourself that the Tao is flowing, that you are involved in that flow, that "home" is as close as your heart.

Do the things in your journal more often.

Fine-tuning your Ch'i balance and uncluttering your view of home is a lot like my listening to a San Francisco Giants baseball game on the radio on my back porch. The dial is set on AM 680. But atmospheric conditions mess up the reception, so that I have to occasionally rotate the radio and its antenna this way or that to bring the game in clearly. Sometimes the static is pretty intense, and I can barely hear if it was Bonds or Snow who hit that home run. But I know I'm tuned in, and if I just relax, and fiddle a bit, the reception will return soon enough.

The Taoist habits are how we reorient ourselves to eliminate the static. To let the signals of Tao and Ch'i come in clear and true.

You'll find it easier to drop into and maintain a relaxed attitude if you express it with *relaxed actions*. These relaxed actions can take a variety of specific forms, depending on your own makeup. You'll know, or be able to find, what actions work best for you to help you relax and enjoy life.

Quiet times work well with me—when I can get them! Sitting in my favorite chair drinking tea, or riding my bike through the park. My wife, Tammy, gets a professional massage toward the end of every week. It's not cheap, but it's effective, and it keeps Tammy functioning well in her many roles of wife, mother, kindergarten teacher, and companion to her many friends. Other people keep candles lit in the house, particularly in the winter. The flickering flames have a wonderful, calming effect. For others, a long, hot bath at the end of the day does the trick. Or maybe a long, hot shower at the start of the day. Or both! Whatever it takes to calm you, to center you, to remind you that you're home, and give you the "ballast" to carry into your many daily activities.

I know it's difficult to relax in our modern West. We have so many responsibilities, so many needs, so many things claiming our attention that seem important. So if Mt. Emei's two truths about humans lead us to the Taoist habit of relaxing, they also lead us to **a second habit: simplify your life, to make it easier to relax and enjoy being "home."**

Simplifying your life involves pruning things out of it—and not just unhealthy things. Every gardener knows that a tree or bush needs to have some perfectly healthy branches cut off periodically, to keep the plant as a whole healthy and

Cultivate Relaxing Habits

Here's my list. Sit down this week and make your own list.

BARNETT'S LIST	YOUR LIST
Snorkeling	_____
Making and drinking tea	_____
Reading in a favorite chair	_____
Bicycling in the park	_____
Candles, incense	_____
A hot shower to finish the day	_____

balanced. Serious simplification of your life means letting go of good things as well as bad.

Bow out of half or all those good causes you work for. What good is it to save the world if you're unhappy in it? *Relax. Simplify.* Get your own life in order first. Then, gently reach out into a bit larger circle.

Our friends Bob and Susan, even though they both make a good salary, surprised us by fixing up their existing home rather than plunging into a larger, more expensive house (and increased mortgage!) several years ago. Last summer they were able to take their family on a vacation to Europe. They enriched their lives, by choosing not to complicate their living arrangements.

Exploring Ways to Simplify Your Life

Look at your calendar or palm pilot for the last month. How many nights and weekends were you away from home? Circle in green the activities that you most enjoyed; circle in black those that you least enjoyed. Now consider how you could eliminate the black ones and focus on the green ones. **Be ruthless.**

Think back over the past several months. Is there an activity or two that kept you from things you like to do? Some activity that required a whole lot more time or energy than you'd have liked to give it?

What would it take to prune that activity down to manageable size? How could you approach it differently? Is it possible or desirable to cut it out of your life altogether? **Be creative.**

Find a quiet spot and think about your job. How could you streamline your tasks, to accomplish them with more efficiency and fewer crises? Are there ways to schedule or redefine your responsibilities to permit you to accomplish them better?

Now the big question: would a new job simplify your life or complicate it? What type of new job might simplify your life? Is training available to qualify you for such a job? **Be bold.**

Ash and Lou are full of energy and enthusiasm. If we let them, they'd take half a dozen extracurricular sport, music, and drama activities. All good, worthwhile activities. We try to limit them to two each, any given semester, though. Things are busy enough with just two activities beyond school. Our lives would plunge into chaos if we tried to do more. Believe me. We've tried, and it wasn't pretty.

You can easily think of many ways, from major to minor, to simplify your own life and create the conditions where you can relax and enjoy life. Consider whether you really need that promotion that's going to require you and your family to move to yet another city. Decline a dinner invitation every now and then, and spend the time instead with yourself or your family.

Simplify your life, so you can **relax**, and revel in the clear realization that you're home. You're in good shape, nothing serious to fix, and nothing to do but let the Ch'i flow and enjoy the richness of life. Your Taoist habits will keep you on course.

CHAPTER 3

Living in the Seasons

My oldest daughter, Heather, and her friends observe a seasonal cycle of sports. In the summer, she surfs in southern California, and plays volleyball on the beach. In the winter, she snowboards in the Sierra Nevada, and occasionally skis. Spring and fall are big for mountain biking along the American River or in the foothills of the Sierra Nevada. You can tell what season it is by the equipment out in her front room: surfboard or snowboard or mountain bike.

Doubtless you have your own particular sports and customs for each season. This attention to the seasons is a good thing, and is highly developed in the Taoist tradition. There are habits, foods, celebrations, and clothes marking each season of our planet in its yearly journey around our local star. **Living in**

the seasons and celebrating benchmarks as our planet moves around the sun is one of the Taoist habits we in the West can enjoy. Let's take a look at how we can do this more fully, and why it's good for us in the Taoist perspective.

As we've seen, we humans are natural creatures, with the same Tao in us as in the rest of the cosmos, with the same Ch'i flowing through us as through granite and water and redwoods. The universe is our home, and its rhythms are ours, especially the rhythms marking our particular planet and solar system. How could it be otherwise?

Western science knows that all life, including humans, of course, evolved from the same common origin, ancient cells using nucleic acids to replicate in the primordial oceans three and a half billion years ago. Our human blood is remarkably salty, because our grand evolutionary saga began originally with creatures in the sea. Our blood sloshes around to the same rhythms as the oceans of the planet. The waxing and the waning of the moon affects our behaviors and attitudes, as does the cycle of seasons the planet passes through in its grand journey around the sun.

The larger rhythms of our planet, the solar system, and the cosmos are ingrained into our beings. When we acknowledge those larger rhythms, pay attention to them and celebrate them, we are paying attention to our own rhythms. We are "in" our bodies more fully. We are more fully "ourselves." So the progression of Heather and her friends from surfboards to mountain bikes to snowboards and skis signifies one aspect of their participation in the rhythms of the planet. It helps keep them aligned with the cosmos.

Part of the Taoist habit of living in the seasons is experiencing their characteristic temperatures and foods. In this age of heated and air-conditioned homes, offices, and vehicles in the West, we cocoon ourselves in air between 68 and 72 degrees Fahrenheit all year. Our grocery stores have produce flown up from southern countries, so we largely have the same fruits and vegetables all year also.

In the Taoist outlook, the seasons aren't different months on the calendar—they're different ways of living. We need to step out of our "conditioned" air more frequently, and get hot in the summer and cold in the winter. Get in the habit of taking off most of our clothes in the summer, and bundling up in sweaters in the winter. Spend time at lakes and beaches in the summer, and around fireplaces in the winter. Eat salads and fresh vegetables in the summer, and soups and stews in the winter. Drink lemonade and iced tea in the summer, and hot chocolate and hot tea in the winter. Be active and cram lots into the days in the summer, but slow down and retire early in the winter. *Live in the season.*

The great surge in popularity of farmers markets is a testament to the urge to live in the season. The folks thronging farmers markets are all Taoists, whether they know it or not. Do you remember the savage joy of biting into the first tomato of the summer? The first watermelon feast? The first bag of mandarin oranges in the early winter?

Explore Your Own "Progression of the Seasons"

	SPRING	SUMMER	AUTUMN	WINTER
Favorite food	_____	_____	_____	_____
Favorite activity	_____	_____	_____	_____
Favorite music	_____	_____	_____	_____
Favorite place	_____	_____	_____	_____

In addition to the four seasons of our planet, there is another series of planetary cycles that affect us all. For much of human history, the cycles of the moon were important both in culture and agriculture, and were prominently marked and celebrated. The lunar calendar is merely a curiosity of obscure farmers almanacs here in the West, and most of us have to concentrate to articulate the difference between a waxing and a waning moon—don't even ask what phase the moon is in tonight! But in China, with its Taoist outlook, the lunar calendar is still important, and where the moon is in its monthly cycle is fresh in the people's minds.

China is full of picturesque lakes, most crowded with party-size pleasure boats. Every pleasure craft that can be rented is spoken for on the fifteenth day of each lunar month, many months in advance. The fifteenth day of the lunar month, of course, is the full moon. The night of the full moon is a time

The Lunar Cycle

Learn to recognize where we are in the cycle when you see the moon, and whether the moon is waxing or waning.

new moon   *full moon*   *new moon*

waxing   **waning**

to be out under that gorgeous, glowing orb with friends and family, enjoying the evening on the lake.

In traditional Korea, the full moon was a time to gather in your garden with friends, drinking wine, or with family, drinking tea, while nature poems were recited far into the night. One of T'ang Dynasty China's most celebrated poets, Li Po, describes a moonlit night in the Huang Shan mountains:

> *To refresh our sorrow-laden souls,*
> *We drank wine deep into the night,*
> *Its moonlit charm far too splendid for sleep.*
> *But in time the wine overtook us,*
> *And we lay ourselves down on the innocent mountain,*
> *The heavens for cover, the earth for pillow.*

What could you do to mark the full moons here in America? You might have some special event or activity to celebrate the occasion. Our Barnett family has a tradition of all sleeping out in the front room every full moon. We drag out our sleeping mats and pillows and quilts. Before retiring, Tammy and I force the kids to take a walk, to see the huge moon rising over the eastern horizon. We point out how the moon is so big on the horizon, and so small when it's overhead, and why its size appears to change so dramatically. (Short answer: even scientists aren't sure why!)

We return to the front room after our moon-viewing, read *Calvin and Hobbes* and play gin rummy for a while in candlelight, then snuggle into our row of bedrolls. It's fun; the kids eagerly look forward to it, because, truth be told, they really don't love sleeping all by themselves in their own separate bedrooms night after night, like most of us do in the prosperous West. This is a bit like camping. Something different, a family occasion. Best of all, Dad wakes up in the middle of the night (hey, when you're in your late fifties, you'll understand about waking up in the middle of the night) and gets to see his kids bathed in moonlight flooding through the west-facing windows. Moonlight is even nicer than candlelight, which is why those party boats in China are all reserved for the fifteenth of every lunar month.

Other cosmic benchmarks you might celebrate are the solstices and equinoxes. These, of course, are solar holidays, connected to the journey of our planet around our local star. Many of us aren't too sure what the devil a solstice or equinox is. For the record, the summer and winter solstices mark the longest and shortest daylight hours of the year, respectively. The equinoxes are the halfway marks, when day length and night length are balanced ("equinox" in Latin means "equal night"). In the northern hemisphere of the planet, due to the tilt of the planet on its axis, our part of the earth is tilted toward the sun maximally on June 21-22, the summer solstice. And tilted away from the sun maximally on December 21-22, the winter solstice. The days begin to lengthen after the winter solstice, and daylight hours catch up with night hours on March 21-22, the vernal equinox. After the ensuing summer solstice, daylight hours begin to shorten, and night length catches up with day on September 21-22, the autumnal equinox.

Here in Valley Oaks Village, we celebrate the winter solstice with a festive parade, where all march with lit candles to the Common House, and an elder talks about the long nights of winter having peaked, and the light of summer beginning to return at this point in our planet's circuit around the sun. Jay tells his story about the sprite who was eating away the sun, a very traditional local tale with Tibetan roots. The kids in the community make a hell of a commotion to scare away the sprite. Then we party the rest of the long evening.

It's not particularly important what you do, but it's good to somehow mark the occasion of the solstices and equinoxes, in a way that seems appropriate to you and your situation. A

Celebrating Solstices, Equinoxes, Full Moons

BARNETT EVENTS   YOUR EVENTS:

	FULL MOONS	EQUINOXES	SOLSTICES
front-room sleep-outs	_____	_____	_____
table of ancestor photos	_____	_____	_____
neighborhood candlelight	_____	_____	_____
walks in the moonlight	_____	_____	_____

family gathering? Candles? Poetry? Whatever you do, it reminds us that we're part of a much larger cycle, that natural rhythms occur in the universe and in us.

Traditional China had a very interesting solar calendar, which has been largely superseded in modern China by our Gregorian calendar. In this traditional calendar, the solar year was divided into twenty-four *Jie Ch'i* intervals ("breaths" or "knots"), of approximately two weeks each. These twenty-four "breaths" were of course grouped into four groups of six, each group corresponding to one of the four seasons. The two-week intervals were given names, using descriptive terms having to do with either the climate or the agricultural cycle. So in traditional China, people would say to each other, "Let's take up this business on the fifth day of Frost Descends" (the interval beginning October 23), or "I'll ship the fertilizer on the first day of Insects Awaken" (the interval beginning March 5). This traditional solar calendar aligns time with the planetary benchmarks of season and agriculture in the northern hemisphere, reminding everyone that we humans are part of this flow of seasons, that our crops, too, are dependent on "The Rains" (March 19) and "Small Heat" (July 7).

I like this solar calendar. It places us humans squarely where we in fact are, in the middle of the natural world. What does June mean to us Westerners? A few know that it's named after a Roman family, but what in the world does a Roman family have to do with the middle of the summer? What does October mean? A few know that it's Latin for the "eighth" month, but as a matter of fact, in our Gregorian calendar, it's not the eighth but the tenth month. No wonder we Westerners are so confused about time and our place in the universe!

I keep a summary of the traditional Chinese solar calendar (Appendix 2) on the wall in our kitchen, and mark off on a covering plastic sheet when we pass from one "breath" to the next. Recently, I've designed a fine-wood circular version of the calendar, with a lever that is moved around the circle from one interval to the next. This version is more attractive, and better reflects the cyclical nature of the passage of our planet around our local star. Keeping track of which "breath" we're in reminds me of these larger rhythms, and our integral participation in them.

The names of the intervals in the traditional solar calendar work for northern China along the Yellow River, of course.

Making Your Own Solar Calendar

Tear out or photocopy the traditional Chinese solar calendar in Appendix 2 and put it on your fridge or somewhere handy.

As you check off the intervals over the next year, come up with your own name for each, one that works for the climate and natural cycles in your part of the world.

Write your new name beside the traditional Chinese name for the interval.

*Next year, collect your twenty-four names into your own **nontraditional solar calendar,** and use this to keep track of your progression through the seasons.*

They may not work very well for Dubuque or Baton Rouge. Make up your own names for the intervals, appropriate to where you live! (When I ask my students to do this, they come up with some really interesting interval names. "Partying Begins!" and "Clamp Down for Finals," for example.)

CHAPTER 4

Continuity with Your Ancestors

How do you feel about your parents? Do you respect them? Like them?

I ask because there's an interesting feel to many homes here in America. Photos of the kids are everywhere, sprouting from every bookshelf and corner and wall, especially hallways. But you have to really look to find an image of those kids' grandparents, and often in vain. Partly this is simply due to our being overwhelmed with kids' portraits from school and sports teams, which roll in inexorably year after year and demand to be placed somewhere. But I get a curious impression from most contemporary American homes that our culture practices "kid worship," in contrast to the "ancestor worship" of traditional China.

In Taiwan and Korea, more so than modern China, department stores have the large, burnished, upright wooden chests with doors that open out and reveal interior shelves. These are ancestor altars, where photos of the family's deceased immediate ancestors are kept, along with flowers and incense sticks. In traditional China, each ancestor for three or more generations back would be represented primarily by a wooden tablet of cypress or juniper, before which the family performed daily rites involving offerings of food, wine, and incense.

Each of these tablets contained part of the ancestor's spirit, imparted by Taoist priests in the ancient burial ritual. The priest dips a brush in blood (or red ink), the surviving family members breathe on the brush, and the "animated" brush touches the tablet, imparting the Ch'i of the ancestor into the tablet itself. "I mark your eyes, and your eyes see," the priest proclaims. "I mark your heart, and your heart beats. I mark your mouth, and your lungs breathe."

Ch'ing Ming

One of the most festive holidays in China, even today, is Ch'ing Ming, "Pure and Bright," the fifth "breath" in the traditional solar calendar. Falling around April 5, this springtime festival centers on a family trip to the burial site of the ancestors, where the graves are swept and spruced up, after which the family pays homage to the ancestors and enjoys the beautiful spring weather. In Honolulu even today, the old Chinese cemetery in Manoa Valley above the university is thronged with Chinese families on Ch'ing Ming honoring their ancestors.

We Westerners have called these activities "ancestor worship," reflecting our own view that when you bow and light candles at an altar, you are, by golly, worshipping. But this term is misleading. The Chinese are not worshipping their ancestors, but rather showing them devout homage. They are honoring their ancestors, acknowledging that the ancestors are responsible for the current family's being on the planet.

Beyond this, there are definite practical reasons for showing respect for the ancestors, in the Taoist view. The collective souls of the ancestors constitute a vital resource that can aid—or harm—the fortunes of the living family, depending on the ancestors' predilections. In Taoist cosmology, each human is constituted of several souls, some of them of heavenly nature (*hun,* meaning "cloud soul") and some of them of earthly nature (*p'o,* meaning "bone soul"). When an elder dies, some of the three *hun* souls go to the collective repository of ancestral *hun* souls. The seven *p'o* souls go back to the earth. Both the *hun* and *p'o* souls' Ch'i energy can affect the fortunes of the living family. So it's prudent and important for the living to show respect and proper behavior toward the ancestors, including the selection of a suitable burial site.

Do I believe in ancestral souls? I'm not sure. But I am sure that our ancestors ought to be acknowledged and honored, in

Got a Problem with a Parent?

Who doesn't?

But think about the world that parent grew up in. Were there some tough and demanding aspects to that world? Was it expected for a parent to spend time with the kids? To show them overt affection?

What inner demons was your parent wrestling with? Did your parent have any community or family or personal resources to help cope with their problems?

Can you accept your parent for who they were, weaknesses and all?

Are you a perfect person?

Do you hope your kids and friends accept you for who you are, weaknesses and all?

view of their role in bringing us to our current family. As a father of four, I know how incredibly challenging and demanding it is to raise kids and keep food on the table and a roof over our heads. No matter if my parents and their parents were or weren't ideal parents according to the expectations of early twenty-first-century American society. The fact is that they brought kids into the world and raised them. That's a feat. So I honor them, and teach my kids to do the same.

Honoring the ancestors is a Taoist habit for the modern West that reminds us of our dependence on our ancestors, and the reverence we owe them, whether they were

saints or scoundrels. We are not independent, or unconnected. We stretch way back in time, century upon century, and are the direct result of considerable devotion, commitment, and sheer luck in surviving the vicissitudes of existence. That's an incredible legacy to acknowledge and celebrate.

How you honor your ancestors is up to you. You may feel that just getting a photo of your parents and grandparents onto a bookshelf is a lot. You may have issues with a parent. Remember—we're not talking popularity here, or awards for good parenting. We're talking about continuity, connecting with a family past that goes way back. Just looking through old family photo albums with the kids will work, like Dagwood Bumstead in the *Blondie* comic, above.

You can get more elaborate, if you wish. On Ch'ing Ming, lunar New Year, and sometimes the summer and winter solstices, we put a small table into a corner of our front room. We cover it with fine linen, and put photos of our departed family members on it, as far back as we have photos. Candles and a small chime are put beside the pictures, along with seashells and whatever little things the kids want to add. Several nights in a row the family gathers informally around this table. We talk about the ancestors as we look at the photos, telling stories about them (the funnier the better). Sometimes we get misty-eyed, particularly when the kids talk about their older sister, Holly, whom we lost four years ago. But mainly it's a celebration of the ancestors, their quirks and lovable habits. Then Ash and Lou light the candles, and one of them rings the chime. And that's it. We leave the table up for a week or so, then I take it down.

Some of my most prized possessions are articles that I inherited from my parents. I still wear some of my dad's shirts. (Boy, did they make shirts better then! These shirts are more than three decades old, but you'll rarely see a button coming off them.) The tea set that my mom inherited from her parents sits in an honored spot on a shelf of our home, and we take tea in it on special occasions. My brother and sisters and I had a prolonged but friendly tussle over who would inherit

---

Reminders of the Ancestors

Search your attic and closets.

Do you have anything that belonged to your parents or grandparents? Aunts or uncles?

Dust it off and bring it out into your daily living space. *If it's functional, use it.*

Tell your kids or friends about it. And about the ancestor you inherited it from.

Balancing the Picture

Sit down with a nice piece of paper, a pen, and a photo of your parents.

Think of your childhood, as far back as you can remember.

List five or so things your mom and dad did right.

Things that showed courage or discipline or an understanding of right and wrong. Things they did for you or your siblings. Perhaps some things that made you laugh or enjoy life.

Put the list beside the photo on a shelf or table in your living space. *Leave it there for a month, and be aware of it as you go about your life.*

our mom's skillet in which she fried her incomparable fried chicken. My sister ended up with the honors, and it makes me happy to think of her continuing Mom's tradition. When I wear Dad's shirt, or serve tea from Mom's tea set, it makes me feel good. Ancestral Ch'i? I don't know. But I like it.

In this day and age, it's unusual to have inherited a home or piece of land where your ancestors resided. If you have, then you should consider continuing the tradition of your family living or working there. I realize that economic factors may dictate otherwise, but be aware that there is an element of "honoring the ancestors" to be considered, if you're taking a Taoist approach. If you must dispose of the land or the home, honoring the ancestors will surely be a strong consideration in deciding to whom you will sell the property. What any possible new owners plan to do with the property should be a factor in your decision.

On the other hand, the Tao flows. Just because your dad was a carpenter doesn't mean you have to be a carpenter and use his tools. What's important is to keep the family line going, whether it involves having kids yourself, adopting kids, or helping raise and influence your brother's or sister's kids, or your cousin's kids. Honoring the ancestors is being involved in your family line, which doesn't necessarily mean following exactly in your ancestors' footsteps.

A haunting tale related in *Peking Story* by David Kidd (1988) illustrates a situation where the ancestors put a very difficult duty into living hands. Kidd married into a very old aristocratic North China family, in the 1940s. An ancestor of this Yu clan, back in the Ming dynasty, had been an official in the court of the Hsuan Te emperor when a palace loaded with gold objects burned. Shortly thereafter, a tribute shipment of red copper arrived from Burma, and another of ground rubies from Turkestan. The ancestor persuaded the emperor to cast a series of bronze incense burners from the gold, copper, and rubies.

The grateful emperor gave fourteen of the masterful incense burners to the Yu ancestor, who took them straight from the casting fires and immediately put a smoldering charcoal brick in each, so that the burners never cooled. In their warm state, they glowed with an unearthly molten fire, surfaces glimmering of rubies and gold. For five hundred years Yu family members had faithfully replenished the burners with fresh charcoal every three days, before the former piece burned out, keeping the incense burners glowing with their original Ming dynasty casting luster. Not for five hundred years had they cooled and taken on the dull, brassy look of everyday bronze.

Kidd's wife quarreled with the gatekeeper's daughter one day, and the child retaliated by pouring water into the incense burners. Five centuries of dutiful obedience were obliterated, and the burners sat cold and dull in front of the ancestral altar when Kidd noticed them the next morning. The gatekeeper left in shame.

Honor the ancestors. But there's no need to cripple the family's future to slavishly preserve the past. The Tao flows. The ancestors know that.

CHAPTER 5

Getting Physical

If you spend any time in parks these days, you see lots of people exercising. Have you noticed how many of them are jogging with grim determination written all over their hard-set faces? These folks appear to be exercising because it's their duty, the Protestant work ethic applied to body care. This is not a Taoist approach to exercise.

Taoists celebrate life in the way they eat, sleep, and exercise. Exercise is promoting the flow of Ch'i along the course set by Tao—hallelujah! Exercise is celebration of the Tao. You don't have to be grinning like an idiot while you exercise if you're a Taoist—although you sure can be—but you will at least be enjoying yourself. Back in my heavy-bicycling days,

I'd get positively giddy, flying down the road with the wind whipping around my body, trees and rocks and squirrels and birds whizzing by on either side of me. Immersed in the Tao! Ch'i pulsing!

Before we moved into Valley Oaks Village, we lived on a country lane on the outskirts of Chico. Every day a guy would jog by our place. He had on headphones attached to a Walkman on his waist, and he was singing along with rock music at the top of his lungs, arms flailing through the air, doing a very good imitation of a whirling dervish. Celebrating. A good Taoist, whether he knew it or not.

When Tammy and I spent the day in the Jade Emperor Taoist temple in Tainan, on the southern tip of Taiwan, a steady stream of folks flocked to the altar to put vegetables, cooking oil, fifty-pound bags of rice, or their children's clothing on the altar table. The chain-smoking "Redhead" shaman-priest of the temple, clad in shorts and a T-shirt, would bless it all with quick rushes of words and hand movements. The men and women, young and old, who came and presented glowing incense before the various altars prayed for health, prosperity, and long life.

Taoism is very much a "this-world" religion. It identifies the driving force and highest good in existence as the Tao that flows through everything that is. Theologians term this an "immanent" religion, as contrasted to the great "transcendent" religions of Buddhism and Christianity and Islam, with their focus on the afterlife (whether called Nirvana's escape from the wheel of existence, or Heaven's reward for passing the test of this life).

In accord with this "immanent" view, Taoists view the body as partaking of the sacredness of existence. The body is, after all, the expression of the flow of Tao in humans. It is the body which pulses with the Ch'i of humans, winding its dynamic way through the myriad transformations of our existence. Hence the Taoist flavor of the whirling dervish jogging by our old home with his Walkman. Hence the vegetables, cooking oil, and rice bags on the altar in Tainan: they, too, are intimately part of the dance of the Tao, involved with the flow of Ch'i through the bodies of the family members.

In the Taoist view, the body and the spirit are not opposed. They're not even separate. Spirit inheres in the physical. Spirit is one aspect of the physical. Put another way, the physical is the way that Tao manifests itself, and so partakes of the sacred. The Tao permeates everything. Everything that is, is one in the Tao that lies at the heart of existence.

Far from something to be neglected, then, the body is to be nurtured and honored. Nurturing the body is nurturing the Tao. Nurturing the body is nurturing the spiritual aspect of existence. **Healthy diet, adequate rest, and appropriate exercise are spiritual habits for a Taoist.** These habits are not exotic or arcane or strenuous in most Taoist outlooks. They are just common sense, part of an appropriate response to life.

Diet

In traditional China, diet was one aspect of medicine. The material you put into your body is a prime determinant of health. Here in modern America, "preventive medicine" is a new, sometimes suspect, and not well-developed aspect of medicine. Not so in China. From the start, the Chinese realized that health is not something to be fixed when you lose it. Rather, health is something you tend every day, something you nurture so that you *don't* lose it. Healthy food is by far better medicine than drastic measures to deal with the loss of health.

Diet in traditional China was high in grains, fruit, and vegetables, and low in fat and meat. The Chinese people (as opposed to the elite) ate lots of wheat in the north and rice in the south, along with the home-grown fruit and vegetables from their gardens or the village fields. Typically, meat was only eaten during the calendar-inspired festivals, several times a month. This diet, of course, reflects our modern "food pyramid" that you see displayed so prominently in America, and which is followed so rarely here. Especially humorous are the rows and rows of high-sugar breakfast cereals for kids, most with the food pyramid they contradict dutifully printed somewhere on the packaging.

As you can imagine, our modern Western diets, sky-high in meat and processed sugars, knock the flow of Ch'i in our bodies off balance. No wonder so many of us act so strange, from kids to elders. The Taoist view insists that we'd feel better and have a richer life if we paid a bit of attention to our diets. **Lots of grains, fruits, and vegetables, smaller amounts of meat.** It's not complicated, is it? But as you well know, it can be challenging to follow our common sense in today's America, where sophisticated and persuasive advertisements blitz us daily to give in to our cravings for sweets and fats. Resist these exhortations to bad health. Better yet, simply turn off the television conveying them to you. Once you get used to a decent diet, and realize how much better you feel every day, it will get easier. Especially when you realize it's a Taoist habit to eat healthy.

If you're a parent, pass on a healthy diet to your kids. I realize that this is difficult, given the society we live in. But it can be done. One simple habit is to keep healthy foods always available for the kids. Our kitchen table has two staples that are sitting on it 24-7: a bowl of multicolored apples (Ash prefers red, Lou green) and a bowl of dried soybeans. We get the soybeans from a food co-op. They're much tastier than they may sound, and a great source of protein.

Do you suspect that eating healthy means eating bland? Not so. Taoists are devoted to this world and its pleasures, so fine-tasting food is all to the good. The Chinese cuisine that is justly world-famous, rivaled in sophistication only by the French, is the cuisine of the ruling elite. The food of the Taoist people of China (what *Taoist Body* author Kristofer Schipper calls "the real country") is not so elaborate, of course, but is still quite tasty. Regional differences are huge

Treating Yourself to High-Class Fuel

If you're eating healthy:

Congratulations! Keep up the good work.

If you're not:

Congratulations! This is the week you'll start.

Don't *rush out and buy a slug of tofu and blue-green algae.*

Wild-eyed enthusiasm and drastic steps are the stuff of fantasy. The Taoist way is to be modest and real.

Do *cut down gradually on sweets and meats. A bit less each day this week. Less the week after. If your body needs meat, eat it. Just not huge servings two or three meals a day! More fish, less beef.*

Do *eat more fruits and vegetables, especially fresh. Eat an apple every day. Your mom was right about this. Sauté or steam vegetables every day. Butter and garlic and onions to enhance the flavor are fine. Pine nuts add a delicious flavor.*

Do *eat complex carbohydrates (rice, potatoes, yams), but only enough to give you the energy you need to get through the day. No more.*

Aahhhh. You feel better already, don't you?

within Chinese cooking, at the level of the people as well as the elite. But everywhere you find ways to spice things up. Garlic in the north, onions on the coast, peppers in the interior. Simple and healthy Taoist diets can also be delicious and intriguing.

(Arcane Taoist texts speak of Taoist masters subsisting only on dew, or mushrooms, or avoiding grains. This is a fanciful description of very advanced masters. We're dealing with normal people here. Stick to your vegetables and grains. The texts mentioning prohibition of grains probably reflect an old Taoist dislike of the shift from a hunter-gatherer Paleolithic lifestyle to the daily grind of the agricultural lifestyle, which tends to blunt the carefree, celebratory approach to life so important in Taoism. We'll get to carefree, celebratory living even eating grains.)

Sleep

Adequate sleep is also a Taoist habit. The rule is, again, very simple. **When you're tired, rest.** That's it. Easy to remember, isn't it? Putting in long workdays, "burning the candle at both ends," partying through the night—this may seem heroic or fun, but you'll pay for it. When your body needs downtime, then shut down like *Blondie*'s Dagwood, below.

Habitually spurning rest when you need it knocks the flow of Ch'i in your body out of whack. It interferes not just with the flow of Ch'i, but also stresses your immune system, making you markedly more susceptible to both short-term

The Art of Napping

When German photographer Hedda Morrison lived in China in the 1930s, she visited a Taoist community on Hua Shan mountain, near Si'an. She noticed that the Taoist priests there took naps. They hiked, they prepared tea, they napped. They did ceremonial Taoist dances, they cultivated their gardens, they napped.

Activity, rest. Activity, rest.

Go and do likewise.

illness and more fundamental malfunctions, such as heart disease and cancer. It's your life, and the Tao flows no matter what. But be aware of what you're doing, at the very least.

Exercise

Exercise is good, and part of the Taoist habits. It should, of course, be appropriate to your own particular situation. At one extreme, young folks who are bursting with vitality can appropriately exercise strenuously. At the other extreme, old folks who are hoarding their diminishing vitality should exercise gently. And, of course, you have all the gradations in between, including youngsters who shouldn't exercise violently and oldsters who can walk all day. Appropriateness is the key here, being sensitive to your own body's abilities and needs.

But do exercise. The Tao flows—that implies some movement. Stasis is death. We'll get to death later. It's not a bad

Greasing Life's Wheels

Do you exercise regularly?

If so: Congratulations! Keep up the good work.

If not: Congratulations! This is the week you start.

Be modest and real in your actions—the Taoist way.

Begin *by walking or bicycling. Buy good shoes or wheels. Then use 'em. Every day, if possible, or close to it.*

In a park is best.

But around the block is okay.

Early morning is best.

But at lunch or after work is fine.

Notice *the sky and trees and rocks as you exercise.*

Start *short and modest, and gradually extend your time.*

Stick *to it, through the minor sore muscles.*

Breathe deep. Flex your muscles. Groan in ecstasy.

thing. But while you're alive, be alive. As the early TV comedian Jack Paar said, the key question isn't whether there's life after death, but whether there's life *before* death. Exactly. **Appropriate exercise is a Taoist habit because it celebrates the flow of the Tao,** and so "greases" the wheels of life. It promotes the flow of Ch'i.

I should say that, generally, a really good Taoist probably doesn't listen to music while she exercises outdoors, contrary to our whirling dervish friend with his Walkman. Chuang Tze talks about "the music of the earth," and Taoists are very attuned to the music of the natural world. The wind rustling through the trees. Birds caroling and squirrels chattering. Water gurgling over rocks. That's heaven. Tuning in to the music of the world is preferred while you're exercising outdoors. But it's also true that the Tao flows strongly through human-composed music, of course. *Very little is forbidden in Taoism.* Some things may distort the flow of the Tao, may produce markedly imbalanced Ch'i. But if you want a weird Ch'i flow, that's your decision. This applies to Walkmen while jogging.

Outdoor exercising is much, much preferable to indoor exercising. Outdoors, you're surrounded by the abundant and obvious Tao of the natural world, through which Ch'i flows in great pulsing waves, balanced and whole. But if you can't exercise outdoors, then by all means exercise indoors. Take some care, though, that while you're nurturing the flow of Ch'i with indoor exercise, you're not imbalancing it in other ways, such as can often happen if you're listening to extreme music, or the TV news' litany of woes. Sure, the Tao is flowing there also, but it's very often violent resolutions of very imbalanced Ch'i. Take care of yourself. I recommend classical or mellow modern music, if you must have some headphones on. But then, I'm an old fogey.

If you're a parent, pass the celebration of exercise on to your kids. Our neighbors Bill and Debbie are famous for their family bicycle outings into the park many times a week. When their first two boys were young, they'd both sit in the Burley trailer attached behind their parents' bike. Now Jasper is old

Taoist Wheels

Things have changed since I was a kid in the fifties. Then, we had Schwinn's with fat tires, never dreamed of having gears giving a choice of speeds. By the eighties, everyone was on racing bikes, with at least twelve and probably twenty-one gears powering their thin tires.

Now, mountain bikes are the rage, and they ought to be. Every good Taoist ought to have a rugged, lightweight mountain bike with thick, knobby tires and loads of gears. If you don't have one, go buy one this week. With this simple machine, you're able to cycle off-road and through wilderness, splash through streams and up hills, follow the Tao wherever it takes you.

Your only restrictions: *Wear a helmet. Bring plenty of water. Stick to the trails in high use areas.* Lao Tze doesn't dig erosion or tearing up fragile terrain.

enough to be on his own bike; Benjamin will join him soon; baby Jesse in a couple of years. Often Bill takes a whole passel of kids riding with him into the park. Funny, when Tammy and I invite Ash and Lou to bicycle to the park with us, it's not often met with enthusiasm. But when Bill is taking Jasper and Benjamin, it's party time, and our kids can't wait to take off.

The Key Question:

Not *"Is there life after death?"*
But *"Is there life before death?"*

CHAPTER 6

Escaping the Mental Prison

We just spent a chapter examining Taoist practices for taking care of the body. So it's time for a chapter about taking care of the mind, right?

Wrong. It's time for a chapter suggesting that we shouldn't obsess about the mind.

The Taoist view of the mind is that it's one of a dozen or so important organs of the body. That's it. One of a dozen or so. To single it out and spend an inordinate amount of time examining it seems strange. To put it on a pedestal as being worthy of consideration as an equal, against all the other organs lumped together ("mind" versus "body"), and moreover as the preeminent entity of this duality (soul resides in mind; the body is simply the temple in which the soul resides)—this approach has Taoists slapping their knees and rolling on the ground in paroxysms of laughter. How absurd!

But that's what we've done in the West, of course. Maybe it's Plato's fault, with his stories about the soul happily driving its chariot through the heavens, then plummeting to earth to be imprisoned in this earthly body "like a pearl in an oyster." Or maybe it was Descartes' fault, with his catchy phrase "Cogito, ergo sum"—"I think, therefore I am."

Whatever. The notion that we are composed of "mind" versus "body," and that mind is preeminent, the seat of the soul, is nonsense, from the Taoist point of view. Guaranteed to produce an imbalanced society, prone to aggression, driven to rush around the world making war on other folks, produc-

---

The Classic Western Perspective

"Man is the measure of all things." —PROTAGORAS

"Cogito, ergo sum." (I think, therefore I am.) —DESCARTES

The Taoist Perspective

"I am an old man and have known a great many troubles, but most of them never happened." —MARK TWAIN

"Except during the nine months before he draws breath, no man manages his affairs as well as a tree does."
—GEORGE BERNARD SHAW

ing more lawyers than gardeners, and putting more people in prisons than in colleges.

In the Taoist tradition, the center of the body is located in the intestines. That seems about right to me. I've known folks with some pretty serious mental problems, but they were otherwise healthy. Some of them robustly healthy. But have a serious problem with your intestines, and you're in misery. Ever seen someone suffering from cholera? If the condition isn't treated quite quickly, it's life-threatening. All sorts of organs are manifestly more essential than the brain. You can live with serious mental problems. But if you've got a problem with your heart, then you have to address it and sooner rather than later. The brain is one among a dozen, remember, and apparently not even one of the more important or vital among those dozen organs.

As I mentioned in the previous chapter, there is nothing that is not rooted in the physical. Soul is one aspect of the physical. Spiritual matters are one among several phenomena associated with the physical. So yes, we should tend to our mind. Keep it healthy. But by all means, don't obsess over it. **Keeping the mind healthy for us Westerners mainly means keeping it in its proper place**—that's our Taoist spiritual habit.

So how do you keep your mind in its proper, Taoist place? Primarily by limiting its share of your time. Whenever you realize that your mind is making a mountain out of a molehill, when your mind is turning into a "worry machine," then simply shift activities. Shifting to a physical activity is most successful. Get up and take a walk around the room, or around the office, or around the world.

A practice that works well for me to escape the mental prison is to simply sit or stroll by a creek. I'm relaxed there, and keenly tuned into the natural scene before me, with all my senses. Soaking up the Ch'i in the surroundings. The dragonflies darting about. The gurgle of the stream over rocks. The redtail hawk screaming upstream. The clouds floating overhead. The acorn woodpeckers gliding from valley oak to valley oak. For me, this is a powerful recharging technique, which invariably quiets what Hinduism calls "the chattering monkey of the mind," and aligns me with the flow of Ch'i in the natural world.

But you don't have to head for a creek. Just a walk around your block, or even around your office, will work. Your mind will calm down, get back to a reasonable state. The new activity needn't be strictly physical. When the worry machine starts to spin out of control, you can focus the mind on something else. Pick up a good book, one that keeps your interest. Even a trashy novel is preferable to letting the worry machine grind on. Make yourself comfortable, brew a cup of tea, and settle into the book.

I am, lamentably, something of an expert on worrying. I used to spend hours worrying about things. All sorts of things. I'd wake up at night, worrying whether there'd be enough *Paramecium* for lab tomorrow. Whether it might rain later in the week and spoil my field trip. Whether I shouldn't be shifting funds from my savings account to my market-rate account. Spend an hour, sometimes two, with it churning through my brain. Toss and turn on the bed, getting completely tangled up in my mind.

I wouldn't be surprised if there's not some genetic component to this tendency to worry about things. Whatever, we need to realize it's a sickness. Not a big fat life-threatening sickness, but a distortion. I still occasionally wake up and begin to worry about something in the middle of the night. But now I just utter some profane exclamation, laugh at myself, and say to myself, "There you go again. What an idiot. Get a grip, Barnett!" This sophisticated technique has resulted in my cutting the frequency and duration of my "worry sessions" at night considerably.

At least I'm in good company so far as worrying goes. "I am an old man and have known a great many troubles," Mark Twain said, "but most of them never happened." Even Thomas Jefferson was afflicted: "How much pain they have cost us," he lamented, "the evils which have never happened."

Another aspect of limiting the "share" of our attention given to the mind is to limit our time in the world of human artifice, products of the mind. The Internet, video games, and television shows are complete inventions of the human mind, their electronic aspect limiting their content drastically, cutting them off from the rich sensory array of the "real" world. They are crammed with the abstract, verbal/visual Ch'i of humans, but have almost nothing of other aspects of human

Liberating Yourself from the Electronic Bully

Do you spend more than an hour a day of your free time in front of a TV or computer screen?

If so: great news! This week is the week you liberate yourself from the tyranny of the screen.

Remember: *you're not eliminating entertainment from your life, just switching to healthy, richer entertainment.*

Each day this week, put a timer beside your TV or computer. Set it to sixty minutes. When it rings, turn off the machine and get yourself outside, rain or shine.

Choose among the following:

Take a walk.

Take a ride on those Taoist mountain-bike wheels you bought last week.

Drive to a mountain or a beach.

Buy a point-and-shoot camera and specialize in creeks or clouds or classic cars or cute guys.

Go to a grocery store. Buy lobsters or pork tenderloin. Snag a cookbook on the way home. Spend the evening preparing a scrumptious meal. Surprise your family with it, or invite a friend to share it with you. Over the meal, talk about the real world.

Ch'i, and nothing whatever of the Ch'i of other creatures, or of the natural world.

Hours spent in front of the computer or TV, or playing video games, are hours closeted in the abstract verbal/visual corners of the human mind. No wonder study after study shows that kids and adults get screwed up by hours of video games and television. It's similar to eating nothing but one kind of food. To stay healthy, we need to interact with the Ch'i of trees and streams and mountains and air and birds and clouds. To neglect this "other" Ch'i and spend hour upon hour locked up in abstract products of the human mind is to starve yourself. It's an unhealthy mental diet. We need to limit our time in these worlds of video games and television and the Internet, and stick to our resolve.

Historical Perspective

Getting all wrapped up in strictly human affairs is quite a common human tendency, of course. Just about every society has a class that focuses only on the human sphere. In traditional China, this class was the Confucians. And in China, as in most human societies, these people had (and still have) the upper hand, forming the ruling elite. But it wasn't always this way in human history. Go far enough back, and you get to cultures immersed in the Tao, people in touch with the natural world and honoring it. Archaeological evidence indicates that this Taoist approach was still preeminent in the Neolithic cultures of the Yang-shao and Lung-shan along the Yellow River. Opulent tomb furnishings of prominent women suggest matriarchal societies in China's past, consistent with the Taoist appreciation of the yin element.

But in China's Bronze Age, the patriarchal, mind-exalting aspect of society began to wax. In time, this faction hitched its fortunes to the Confucian philosophy, and has been in control of the ruling central authority in China for the past three thousand years, whether in a feudal, imperial, or Communist regime. Taoism, with its appreciation of the richness of reality, the balance of yin and yang, and the proper place of humans, has been the view of the *people* for these three thousand years. The Taoist populace has gone its own way in the countryside and the villages—the "real country," as Kristofer Schipper puts it in *Taoist Body*—while the imperial Confucian juggernaut ruled the cities and the empire.

Very much the same thing happened in the West, but the conquest of the "mind is paramount" faction was even more complete, thanks to Plato and Descartes and Christianity. As a result, the old outlooks in the West, which celebrated the earth and accorded respect to the feminine, were driven thoroughly underground, and often to extinction—the Druids, the Greek mystery religions, the fertility cults, animism, most recently the Native Americans' shamanism. Similar to the ancient Western religions, Taoism, unlike them, has miraculously survived into modern times in China. Praise be!

Evolutionary Perspective

You've got to wonder: what is the biological explanation for this all-too-common tendency for humans to get imprisoned in their minds, for the worldwide ascendancy of humans who exalt the mind above all other aspects of humanity?

The answer is reasonably clear to a scientist. All plants and animals have specific adaptations that permit them to excel in their habitats, to outcompete other creatures for the resources they need. It may be the ability to survive and prosper with little water, or to blend into their environment, or to digest poor-quality forage efficiently, or to develop and deliver devastating toxins to their prey or their enemies, or sometimes to simply be the biggest or the swiftest creature around. For humans, our key trait that permits us to survive and flourish is clearly our brain and its ability to think. To abstractly imagine situations and prepare for them. To devise novel ways to hunt and hide and court and protect our young. Our mind is, in fact, key to our prosperity as a species.

So it's not surprising that there is a tendency for us humans to spend a lot of time "in our heads." In our evolutionary history, the active exercise of our mind was critical to our survival. What has happened is that this trait has been exaggerated through time, so its effectiveness has, in fact, been compromised by unforeseen side effects, particularly in evolutionarily new settings—such as cities.

This phenomenon of a beneficial trait being exaggerated, and becoming detrimental to the prosperity of the descendants and the species at a later time, is well documented in the fossil record. The Irish elk's antlers became so huge in the Pleistocene epoch that the metabolic cost of producing them year after year, along with their weight, and conspicuousness to predators, outweighed their early advantages. Further back in time, the early Mesozoic reptiles radiated into gigantic dinosaurs, their sheer size giving them advantages over competitors and prey. When asteroids rained on the earth sixty-five million years ago, though, the resultant decline in plant production starved these giants with their enormous demands for forage, leading to their extinction. A trait contributing to their success became a liability in a changed situation. Only the tiny late-Mesozoic mammals, able to live on detritus and seeds, survived through the long food-starved catastrophe of the asteroids, and soon began to radiate into the newly vacant, larger-size niches themselves.

Our human brains were key to the survival of our ancestral hominid apes several million years ago, and to our consequent prosperity on the planet. But there are side effects to having large brains with very complicated neural circuitry, side effects that may be very serious in changed ecological or social situations. We can think well, but we also worry. We get tangled up in our heads and our imagined worlds, and separated from the natural world, our home. We get lost. Disoriented. Some of us badly disoriented. Some of us become depressed and commit suicide. A few of us slaughter our fellows, even sometimes our spouse and children, tragedies hardly known in creatures without large brains. Our large brains let us compose symphonies and sing gorgeous arias, but they also lead us to drop bombs that incinerate our fellow humans and poison the sacred earth.

We cannot eliminate our large brains, even if we wished to. We must accept our minds. But we should keep ourselves from being imprisoned in our minds. We can adopt the Taoist habit of putting our mind in its proper place—one organ among a dozen or so. **Our minds are important to our evolutionary success, but not paramount in our bodies.** Not more important than our hearts or our intestines. One among a dozen.

Meditation

What is the role of meditation in escaping the prison of the mind? Meditation was not part of early religious Taoism of the Tian Shih movement. (See Appendix 3 for a brief description of different schools and levels of Taoism in China.) Nor did meditation have any place in the early myriad expressions of the Taoist outlook in Chinese culture or folk Taoism. It was not until Buddhism became an important factor in China in the fourth century A.D. that meditation became a *priestly* practice in some of the new, "reform" schools of religious Taoism. Even then, meditation was merely one of several methods that a Taoist priest might specialize in to achieve oneness with the Tao. Never was meditation a practice that the common people engaged in. Who had time or opportunity in China to sit still, close their eyes, and be alone in a quiet spot?! And anyway, there was the suspicion that meditation was, in fact, a way of exploring the prison of the mind, rather than a practice to escape it.

Because of these various considerations, I don't consider meditation an everyday Taoist habit. Perhaps, for some folks in other traditions, some forms of meditation can, in fact, provide an avenue to "quiet the chattering monkey of the mind." For those folks—have at it, and congratulations. I have several Buddhist friends who meditate regularly, one who was a monk for over a decade, and they are wonderful people that I respect and whose company I enjoy. But the distinctively Taoist approach to escaping the prison of the mind involves routes other than meditation, routes more concerned with the flow of Tao in the natural world.

So, to escape the mental prison so common in the West, we can limit our worry time, and limit our time in the world of human artifice. On the positive side, we can plunge ourselves more frequently into the wider world—the world of family and physical activities and parks and gardens and flowing streams. This, of course, brings us back to the first Taoist habit: *immersion in the Tao.* Having a healthy life participating in everyday Taoist habits is the best way to escape the mental prison.

CHAPTER 7

Celebrating Your Guides

If you choose to travel on holidays, you at least know what you're getting into, right? Long lines, full flights, harried ticket agents, the whole thing. Even if you're traveling out of the country, to Europe, you're generally aware of when the big holidays are, and what days to avoid. Now, one reason Kyle and I like to travel to obscure places in Asia is that the cultures are so different from our Euro-American culture at home. But sometimes that intriguing "otherness" of Asia turns into a travel nightmare.

Kyle and I made the mistake of flying into Taiwan several years ago on what turned out to be, unknown to us, the fifth day of the fifth lunar month—Double Five. We had planned what we thought was a fairly easy day of travel. Arrive in Taipei from Japan, immediately get a plane to Tainan on the southern end of the island, and be fresh the next day for exploration of that city's famous plethora of Taoist temples.

Or so we thought.

As it turned out, everyone goes to their family home on Double Five, also called the Dragon Boat Festival, so, of course, every plane going anywhere in the country from Taipei was booked solid. Leaning on my rusty Chinese, we struggled through Taipei to the bus station. No room on the express bus to Tainan. The best we could do is the local milk run—well, this is China, so the "tea run"—to Taichung, in the middle of the island. Okay. The bus was incredibly crowded, and I'm not just talking humans, either. There were nearly as many chickens and pigs on the contraption as humans. (Two guesses what the traditional meals are for the Dragon Boat Festival.)

We arrived in Taichung late afternoon. No room on even the tea run to Tainan, of course. Try the train station. We plunge ourselves and our packs into Taichung's crowded streets, finally finding the train station forty minutes later. We scored the last two seats to Tainan. Elated, we scrambled aboard just as the train chugged out of the bedlam of the station.

There were fewer pigs and chickens on the train, but a lot more people. The aisles were crammed with "standing room" passengers. I was too exhausted to eject the sullen-looking young soldiers from what I thought were our seats. So we stood in the aisle for another three hours. I struck up a conversation with a local fellow, who ejected the soldiers from

Lung Shan Temple, Taipei

our seats himself. We sank into them like pigs into mud. After only ten minutes in hog heaven, Tainan arrived. My new friend advised us where to get a room—indeed, the only place that might still have a room, he said. Another forty-minute walk with our backpacks, all restaurants closed, since we're approaching midnight. We had barely eaten all day. Much to our surprise, there actually was a room in the cheap hotel, and both backpacks hit the floor with a clunk simultaneously, two seconds before two bodies hit the beds, also with clunks. We were asleep instantly, and didn't even get close to waking up for t'ai chi in the park the next morning.

Beware traveling on Chinese festival days. And there are a

lot of them. The Chinese are always celebrating something, it seems. The lunar calendar is chock-full of special days that require travel to a family gathering, special food, and often some public ritual in the local temple. Most of us have heard of Chinese New Year, and the Lantern Festival. The Dragon Boat Festival ("Double Five") was certainly etched into my consciousness—and bones—after the above experience.

But there are many other festivals. Some of them are centered on "cults" (in the anthropological, benign sense of the word) in the local temple—patron saints peculiar to a particular village or region. Others celebrate mythical or historical figures of national renown, such as the Queen Mother of the West (Hsi Wang Mu), or Kuan Kung, the betrayed general of the Three Kingdoms Romance two thousand years ago, or Ma Tze, the young virgin, patron saint of sailors and women, who ascended to heaven one afternoon a mere thousand years ago. To this roster, Taoist priests add celebrations of their own, strictly religious figures, such as the birthday of Lao Tze, author of the *Tao Te Ching,* or a day set aside for Chang Tao Ling, the founder of religious Taoism in the Han dynasty nearly two thousand years ago.

These celebrations remind the Chinese of the long and rich reach of their culture. They remind the Chinese of what is important, and the many heroes and patron saints who embody the drama and the magic of existence. Note that these festivals don't celebrate figures known for virtuous living. The official, state-sponsored cult of Confucius pays homage

Ma Tze, patron saint of sailors and women

to virtuous living. The Taoist populace celebrates magic, awe, and wonder—the side of existence that adds spice and zest to life, the side of life that you spin tales about to regale your friends and kids.

We have plenty of holidays in the West, but it strikes me that they're a little thin on the magic side. I suppose it's important to celebrate George Washington, Martin Luther King, July 4, and pilgrims. But gosh—what happened to the magic, awe, and wonder of life in Western civilization? **So a Taoist**

Childhood Wonders

If not often as adults, then surely most of us experienced wonder frequently as children. Think back to your most wonder-filled Halloween night or Christmas morning. Sit down and write a short story describing it, and your feelings. Show the story to a family member or friend, and ask them to share an equivalent story from their childhood.

Savor the remembered wonder, joy, and awe.

habit for us in America is to celebrate our guides to the colorful wonder of existence. Those guides may be Chinese or they may be Western, but celebrating their unusual lives and adventures enriches our own lives, reminds us that there's more to life than being "good" and obeying our parents and our government.

Do we have any of these holidays in America now? Maybe Halloween, but it's mainly for children and college students, these days. Christmas and Santa Claus are definitely children-centered. Adults are expected to be beyond such "silliness." Are we adults beyond the celebration of wonder so prevalent in Chinese culture?

The only cult figure we have in America that corresponds to the rich assemblage of cult figures in China is . . . Elvis. Seriously. Who else inspires thousands of adults to stand in the rain at Graceland on his birthday? To dress up like him and reenact his legendary performances? What other Ameri-

Halloween suspends the daily grind.

can continues to be glimpsed in malls and along roadways decades after his death? Talk about concentrated Ch'i persisting after a person's demise!

Elvis was certainly no paragon of virtuous living. But he made us feel alive and young, and it was okay to scream and faint in his presence. *Now there's something to celebrate!* Should we declare Elvis's birthday a national holiday? No!! Don't let the government get hold of Elvis. The legislature and the governor will have him all tamed down and as dull and venal as themselves in a year. No, the holiday celebrating Elvis should just bubble up from the people. It's already happening. The best thing that could happen would be for the stuffy, virtuous government to *outlaw* any celebration of Elvis. That would ensure a full-out blooming of national sentiment to get the zaniness, the passion for life that was Elvis onto its proper, nationally celebrated stage: a people's holiday.

And after that, we'll start to work on Marilyn Monroe.

But you don't have to wait for a holiday honoring Elvis and his rich concentration of Ch'i. Pick whatever guides and "patron saints" speak to you. Are you a committed feminist? Get crazy on Susan B. Anthony's birthday, or maybe the day Elizabeth Cady Stanton read her Declaration of Sentiments at Seneca Falls in 1848. Do you think alcohol abuse needs to be addressed? Celebrate Carrie Nation on the day she took the ax to that bar in Kansas, perhaps with ample servings of lemonade and iced tea. Are you a hard-core environmentalist? Start a tradition of hiking into your favorite camp-spot on John Muir's birthday and raise hell there. I admire Thomas Jefferson as a stellar blend of scientist, statesman, farmer, and writer. So, for a while, I had friends over on his birthday, and read parts of the Declaration of Independence while we drank the West Indies rum he liked to drink. If you're a Buddhist, then join millions worldwide in celebrating Buddha's birthday. Lighting candles and ringing bells may be more appropriate than drinking, here—but it's your celebration.

Many of the altars in Chinese temples are for local historical figures who did exceptional things and were admitted into the ranks of local "saints." What is honored and celebrated at their altars is not just they as people, but the exceptional Ch'i that flowed through them. The Chinese think that

John Muir celebrated Yosemite Park.

exceptional concentrations of Ch'i don't just disappear upon the person's death. They persist, and even centuries later these concentrations, these persistent Ch'i nodes, can be called upon for help. Hence the local "cults," so prevalent throughout China.

So, start your own cult of local figures who were exceptional in your town or region. You'll need some perspective on these figures, to judge the potency of their Ch'i, so they should be deceased, generally. They don't have to have been "religious" or "holy" people—not many of the Chinese cult

Celebrating Wonder

Make a list of people that could fill you, as an adult, with wonder and awe. Possibilities: *Elvis, Frank Sinatra, Babe Ruth, Harriet Beecher Stowe, Jack Kerouac, Gerard Manley Hopkins, Jimi Hendrix, Janis Joplin, St. Francis of Assisi, Jack Kennedy.*

Your list will be different, of course. Start it right here, and remember: we're talking passion for life here, not virtue or nobility.

Now decide which one or two speak most intensely to you. Find their birthday. Start planning today for a birthday party that celebrates not their achievements, not their public recognition, but their passion for life, *their heart-filling pursuit of their bliss.*

Should the party be outside or inside?

What type of food and drink is especially apt? Be sure to have plenty of it!

Invite friends who can appreciate your person and their passion for life.

When the birthday arrives, relax and celebrate!

figures were. They don't even have to have been likable or virtuous. But they do have to have been people with exceptional Ch'i flowing through them. Did someone stop a housing development that would have destroyed a beautiful meadow in your region, and turn it into a park instead? Honor that. Did someone sit in a tree for months to protest

Mini-Celebrations Through the Year

Find all the birthdays of the people you previously listed that fill you with wonder. Mark them on your calendar or palm pilot. Underline them in red or highlight them.

When each birthday arrives, note it and talk about it all day with your family, your friends, your coworkers. Remember the person's zest for life, all day, and smile a lot. Play the person's music or read their poetry or drink their favorite drink. Let each person on your list light up your day on their birthday.

Life is more fun already, isn't it?

the logging of thousand-year-old redwoods? Honor her. Did someone host a pancake breakfast for needy kids every spring for two decades? Honor him. Did someone found a children's theater where a generation of kids entered the worlds of *Annie* and *The Music Man* and *Scrooge*? Honor her.

When we celebrate these guides, we celebrate the rich Ch'i that coursed through them. We access some of that Ch'i ourselves. We remind ourselves that life itself is a fantastically rich celebration of the myriad and colorful ways that the Tao flows through us and the world. Celebrate!

CHAPTER 8

Accept, Accept, Accept

We live in a country where scores of determined candidates campaign for public office a year before the election. Where professional wrestlers and actors and owners of baseball teams eagerly become governors and presidents. So it's difficult for you and me to imagine a society in which people scorn governmental service.

Yet Chinese folklore is full of stories about talented men who are begged by the emperor to come to court and serve him, throwing their lives into political struggles. Inevitably, the emperor's representative is spurned, with some comment like "Cranes soar thousands of li above the earth. You would have me become a turtle, dragging myself through mud."

Taoists, keenly aware of the propensity for us sensitive humans to get nudged off course into imbalanced Ch'i situations, are not about to get tangled up in the vexing struggles of human affairs. They're much more likely to laugh at the situation than rush in to straighten it out, and most likely of all to simply walk away.

"Making accusations is not as good as laughing," an enlightened "Taoist" Confucius says in the *Chuang Tze*. "And laughter is not as good as letting things follow their natural course. **Be content with what is happening, and forget about change.** Then you can enter into the oneness of the mystery of heaven." In other words: **Accept, accept, accept.**

No doubt about it, the Taoist tendency is to just leave things be, including human affairs. This may seem entirely reasonable and sensible to people in many parts of the world. But here in America, especially here in California, it's shocking. As a child of the 60s in America, I was weaned on political action to "right" social wrongs. And sometimes it worked. The Civil Rights movement certainly led to African-Americans inheriting many of the rights of citizenship long denied them. The anti-war movement certainly had a huge role in persuading Lyndon Johnson not to run for reelection, and Richard Nixon and Henry Kissinger to negotiate for peace in Southeast Asia.

The Taoist lack of interest in remedying social injustice, the lack of passion for social improvement, is one of the hardest things about Taoism for us Americans to understand. But the tendency is clear, and it follows directly from bedrock

Taoist views of reality. The Tao flows. Everywhere. Nothing lacks the Tao. Even imbalanced flows represent a natural situation. Nothing is broken, in need of being fixed. We must accept things as they are.

The *Tao Te Ching* puts it eloquently:

"Do you think you can take over the universe and improve it? I don't believe it can be done. The universe is sacred. You cannot improve it. If you try to change it, you'll ruin it. If you try to control it, you'll lose it."

Rebelling against the world is not an option for Taoists. And that seems to include unjust human situations. Rejecting what is—that's not thinkable. What is, is that way because of its Tao. We are committed to reality, even ugly reality.

What?!? Accept my spouse as he is? But he snores, he smokes, and if I don't watch him like a hawk, he'll cheat on me. Accept the coarsening of human culture as American pop music and videos and fast food sweep across the globe? No way!

I'll admit upfront that this Taoist insistence on accepting things as they are in the world is the hardest thing for me to understand about Taoism. Here are a few considerations that help me make some sense of it.

First, we are asked only to accept that things are as they are. We aren't asked to pretend that they are good, or the best way things could be arranged. The flow of the Tao has nothing to do with good or bad, moral or immoral. These are human judgments, and it's okay to make them, but they're not fundamental to "the way things are." Beyond the observation

Rattlesnakes and Poison Oak

For today only: be nonjudgmental about people, about events. Don't let yourself be disappointed or angry that people do what they do.

Think of people as you would a rattlesnake: are you angry that a rattlesnake acts like a rattlesnake? Are you angry that poison oak is a skin irritant? Of course not. You accept that they are what they are, and just do your best not to brush against them the wrong way. Rattlesnakes and poison oak teach us to be alert and watch our step. Same with humans, today. Wear this attitude for a day, and see how it fits. Next week, wear the attitude two days. The week after, three days.

that the Tao generally favors the emergence of life and its support, there's no particular "good news" for humans in the Taoist outlook. There's certainly no exaltation of moral, virtuous living by humans as a prerequisite to being engaged in the flow of the Tao. Both the thief and the saint can participate in the flow of the Tao, as Chuang Tze points out. "In doing good, avoid fame. In doing evil, avoid punishment. Thus, by pursuing the middle way, you may preserve your body, fulfill your life, look after your parents, and live out your years."

Second, one reason it's wise to accept things as they are is that they won't be that way forever. There's no need to get all worked up over something that's inherently impermanent and bound to disappear in the course of time. The flow of the Tao is incredibly dynamic, and is marked by constant transformations. And it's fair game for you to put your Ch'i energy to work nudging the flow of the Tao in the direction you're more comfortable with.

Is your wife a chain smoker? Accept it, then work to create conditions where you can live with it or eliminate it. That's fair! But you're well advised to accept it, first, not only because it's real and part of the flow of the Tao right now, but also because you're more likely to be successful at changing it if you start with an acceptance of it.

He Drives Me Absolutely Bonkers!

Think of a relative or family member with a trait that drives you nuts.

Did they acquire and cultivate that trait specifically to drive you nuts? Or is it an inherited trait, found also in a parent or aunt or uncle?

Does this make a difference in how you think of the trait? Of the person who has it?

Reflect on the trait. *Does it have a beneficial side? Does it permit the person to achieve things or enjoy things that they might not otherwise?*

Is it necessary for you to be vexed by this person's trait? Is it possible to give the trait to the universe, and get on with your life?

You don't successfully change a person or a situation by rejecting them as completely devoid of meaning. Most of us have learned, from painful experience, that things just don't work that way. You start by accepting the person or situation, and then nudge the flow of the Tao to transform the person or situation in the direction you're comfortable with. Better strategy. A more successful approach, because it starts by accepting reality, and then taking advantage of the dynamic aspect of reality.

Third, the Taoist insistence on acceptance has a lot to do with perspective. Taoism does not elevate humans to the apex of creation. Far from it. Humans are simply another one of "the ten thousand things." Very complex, true. But nothing extraordinary, really. The implication, of course, is that human affairs are not nearly as important as we generally think they are. The Tao flows through all of existence. It's been coursing through this planet for about 4.5 billion years. Life arose 3.5 billion years ago. Trilobites came, dominated the earth, then disappeared. Dinosaurs came, ruled for a hundred million years, then were gone in a geological instant. We humans have been here a very brief 2 million years or so (even interpreting "human" very liberally). There's no reason to think that we'll be here forever. No other creature has, in 3.5 billion years of life on the planet.

It's awfully easy for us to get "stuck" on all the things that are "wrong" in human society. Often we get fixated, and fret and rage about "the war" or "the environmentalists" or whatever else we perceive to be wrong with society. The Taoist tradition suggests that we tone down our anger, our disappointment. Not that we ignore it, but that we balance it. The Tao is flowing in the world. The stars shine in the heavens, creeks flow to the sea, the planet whirls through the grand cycle of the seasons, children play and grow strong, the beauty and exuberance of the world presents itself to you daily. Ig-

Giving It to the Universe

Get a nice piece of paper and a pen. Take a seat. Think of the issue that most infuriates you. Perhaps it's the environmental movement. Perhaps it's the military-industrial complex. Perhaps it's the right-to-lifers. The conservatives. The liberals. Whatever. Write a short essay on what bothers you about this issue. Express how angry it makes you. How vitally important this is to our country, to the world.

Take the paper with your essay and some string to the closest creek or river. Find a stick or branch, and wrap your paper around the branch, securing it with the string.

Walk to the edge of the creek. Watch the water flowing by. Figure out what route it takes to get to what ocean.

Take a deep breath, then toss your issue wrapped around the stick into the creek. Watch your issue get taken up by the flow of the water, and head for the ocean.

Give your issue to the universe, and trust the universe to deal with it, in its own way. Return home, and concentrate more on the positive things in your life.

noring all this, and fixating on one imbalanced aspect of human society, makes you part of the imbalance, part of the problem. *Better to open our eyes wider, to take in more of the awesome universe.*

So your husband snores? Big deal. Think of separate bedrooms. Bad things happen to good people? That makes me angry, and sometimes deeply sorrowful. But it's not a flaw in the universe. It's just the way things are. Endure the rough times, survive the turbulence, and move on. Let the Tao flow in you, even as it hopefully flowed strongly in those good people that suffered bad things.

Note that this Taoist practice of accepting the world as it is does not mean pretending that there is some hidden "meaning" in events that seem otherwise inexplicable or tragic. The

The Way Things Are

Find a spot that intrigues you in a wild area, one not "managed" by humans. Creekside would be an example. Make a habit of going there several times a year, year after year. Observe all the changes that occur there, both cyclical (different birds, leaves coming and going) and linear (high water sculpting the bank). Keep track of these changes in a notebook; memory is slippery!

Note that change is natural and unavoidable. In this spot. In your life. In all human affairs, regardless of how hard we try to escape or mitigate it.

Tao flows according to its own inherent course, and is not interested in "making things happen" for a purpose relevant to humans. Consider an avalanche of snow and ice roaring down upon an alpine scene. Is there a troop of Girl Scouts in that village? That is tragic. But there is no meaning beyond that in it. What if Public Enemy Number One was in the buried village? Say, Osama bin Laden (from the American view) or George Bush (from the Taliban view). That would not change the event or give it a "meaning" or moral. The event is the event. Things happen because things happen. It is our job, as Taoists, to avoid avalanche-prone areas as best we can. To shoulder the tragedies that come our way. And to cleave to the Tao, moving ahead with our lives.

Surely, sometimes the tragedies inherent in life seem too much for us to bear. We in America and in the West are able to successfully shelter ourselves from much of the tragedy that was common in our societies only a century ago, and is still common throughout most of the rest of the world. Infant mortality is relatively low in our society, accidental death is uncommon, advanced warning systems prepare us for hurricanes and winter storms and volcanic eruptions. Yet even we modern Americans are sometimes struck with tragedy. It seems even more shattering to us when it happens, precisely because it is so much less common in our society. It is easy to write "shoulder the tragedy, and cleave to the Tao," but not so easy to actually do it. I speak from experience here.

What helps me to accept tragedy when it strikes my life is to concentrate on the first Taoist habit. When things are agonizingly tough for me, I head for a natural setting, to immerse myself in the abundant Tao there. When my twenty-three-year-old daughter Holly was undergoing radiation therapy for her cancer, I would get up from my desk during the fifteen minutes that radiation was being beamed into her, and walk to nearby Big Chico Creek. I would stand on the shore, watching the water flow by, thinking of Holly, opening up to the flow of the Tao into my life and hers. I didn't pretend that the flow of the creek or the flow of the Tao was going to cure her of cancer. But it helped me, to be there among the creek-side valley oaks and alders and sycamores, the water flowing by, dragonflies coursing up and down the creek. Perhaps it reminded me of the grandeur and drama of life. Reminded me that life was a gift to us. That even in rough times life was a gift, and that participating in the flow of the Tao was what was important. That the Tao flowed, in health and sickness, in life and death.

Holly died in midwinter. We staggered through the rest of the winter, and our short spring. When summer came, Tam and Ash and Lou and I headed for Big Chico Creek again, near our home. The sycamore trees along the creek shed patches of their bark all year long. We collected some of these patches from the bank, and wrote poems to Holly on the smooth underside of the bark. Short, haiku-like poems about

Honoring the Flow of the Tao

Think of a loved one who has died. Somone you really miss from your life.

Remember the good times you shared. The laughs. The adventures. The rich times, full of warmth and life. The strength and dignity with which this person endured hard times. Think of the Tao that flowed strongly through him or her, and through you when you were with this person.

Put a photo of the loved one on a shelf, with a candle beside it. Light the candle when you're around. On a special occasion, put a vase of flowers beside the photo.

Honor the loved one. And the Tao that flowed through this person.

For the next several months, cultivate in your own life the warmth, laughter, and strength of your loved one. Share these with your family and friends. Who knows? Maybe your photo will be sitting beside someone's candle some day.

her life, how much we missed her, and how good it was to think of her with spring all around. Then we waded out into the creek, and gently placed our patch of bark on the flowing water, and gave it to the universe. We stood there in the water and watched as the flow of the Tao carried Holly's poems away from us toward the Sacramento River, and beyond that to San Francisco Bay, and beyond that to the immense Pacific Ocean.

We knew that Holly was a part of that flow.

There are many ways of coping with—of accepting—the rough spots in life. In traditional China, a troubled person would seek out a Taoist priest and ask for help. If the problem arose from an imbalance in the flow of Ch'i, the priest would set a penance for the person, or inscribe a magic talisman to wear, or prescribe a particular diet for the person—whatever was appropriate to rectify the flow of Ch'i to a more harmonious, prosperous course. If the problem was simply a tragedy, the priest would help the person survive it and move on, perhaps with a prescription for a tonic beverage or a tonic diet. Perhaps by gently reminding the person to light candles for the lost loved one at the village temple every day for a year.

As you might guess, there are precious few Taoist priests in the modern West. Perhaps a therapist or counselor might help some of us cope with tragedy. It is generally not the Taoist way to talk or think your way in or out of problems. But a counselor with a Taoist viewpoint might help some of us to come to grips with a tough situation, to accept it as simply a turbulent spot in the flow of the Tao, however tragic, and then to move on.

Lastly, we should realize that the habit of accepting the world as it is pertains to the smooth times as well as the turbulent times. Taoists revel in the sweet gifts of life. You will remember that Taoism is an immanent religion, not a transcendent one. For Taoists, life is a gift, the hard times to be endured, the good times to be savored. The habit of accep-

Making a List, Checking it Twice

Next week, Monday morning, before you begin your day's activities, write down one sweet thing in your life. *Keep the paper in your pocket all day.*

Add one thing to the list every subsequent morning of the week.

Pull the paper from your pocket and remind yourself of the things there several times a day, all week.

Let the sweet things in your life be on your mind as much as the challenges and distractions this next week.

The week after, let the sweet things be on your mind more than the others.

tance enjoins us to drink deeply of the joys of life. Food, drink, friendship, family, sex, sports, picnics, laughter—especially laughter—poetry, parties, moonlit walks—all these and more are important parts of the Taoist life. **Enjoying the sweet gifts of life is a Taoist habit,** part of the habit of accepting the flow of the Tao in the world. And as we explore in the next chapter, acceptance of the sweet things in life gives rise to a characteristic twinkle in the eye of Taoists, a twinkle even amid the harsh lines of tragedy there.

We must try to accept, accept, accept. The Tao is flowing, as it should. It flowed long before we arrived, and will flow long after we leave. It is flowing today, through you. Through me. Through every plant in your garden. Through every rock and creek and living thing in your neighborhood park. That is the important thing to remember. Surely, some aspects of its flow are turbulent. Unjust, from our human perspective. Painful enough to make us weep and wail, sometimes, when that roughness strikes a loved one. Painful enough to carve a piece of your heart out, perhaps for the rest of your life. But the Tao flows. In the world, in us. It flows in the good and sweet things as surely as in the hard things of life. *Accept, accept, accept. All of it.* To do anything less is to turn away from the Tao. And that we cannot do.

CHAPTER 9

The Clown Within

If you're lucky, you have a friend like my buddy A.J., whom I ran into in Beijing just before climbing Emei Shan. You know the sort of person—every encounter is a happening, bringing a smile to your face as you listen to his latest outrageous story. Warming your heart as you hear his laughter cutting through the grim seriousness of our everyday grind. When the warming accent is A.J.'s delicious Southern drawl (he's from Richmond), the effect is particularly heady. It's the A.J.s in our lives that we immediately seek out when we've got great news to share, when we want to laugh and whoop and act outrageous.

Taoists understand this urge, and think it's an important part of life. In no religion or philosophy are whimsy, humor, and the deliberately shocking more common than in Taoism. The sinologist John Blofeld wandered in China throughout the 1930s, when the traditional ways were still strong. He sought out Taoist masters, and spent long hours with them in their Taoist communities. In *Taoist Mysteries and Magic* (1973), he summarizes what he found:

"I can list from firsthand knowledge certain general characteristics of Taoist recluses as I found them: A healthy impatience with tiresome and restricting conventions . . . A ready acceptance of life as it came . . . A readiness to laugh engagingly at mishaps as well as at what they took to be their own inadequacies and follies, so that grumbling and pomposity were scarcely to be found among them."

The following vignettes from the *Chuang Tze* reflect a twinkle in the eye that is rarely absent from a Taoist.

When the Taoist master Chang Wu Tze is faced with a barrage of questions and theories by his anxious disciple, fresh from a lengthy interview with Confucius, he chuckles and shakes his head: "These words would have confused even the Yellow Emperor, so how could Confucius understand them? Moreover, you're too quick to draw conclusions. You see an egg, and immediately listen for the crowing of a full-grown cock. You see a bow, and you look for a roast dove. Let me give you a rough explanation, but don't take this too literally, all right?"

Elsewhere in the *Chuang Tze,* four friends named Tsu talk, and laugh together when they find no disagreement

Sliding

I've observed that it's often a very small leap from absolute bewilderment and outrage at the antics of politicians or sports figures, to a hearty laugh at the sheer nonsense of it all.

Practice sliding over outrage and getting to laughter more often.

Dwell less on the outrage and more on the laughter.

among them. Tsu Yu falls ill, and is visited by Tsu Szu, who finds his friend in horrible shape. "His crooked spine was curled round like a hunchback; his five organs were upside down; his chin rested on his navel; his shoulders rose up above his head; his neckbone pointed to the sky. His body was sick, yet he was calm and carefree. He limped to the well and looked at his reflection and said, Ah! The Maker of Things has made me all crooked like this!"

"Does this upset you?" asks Tsu Szu.

"No, why should it? If my left arm became a rooster, I would use it to herald the dawn. If my right arm became a crossbow, I would shoot down a bird for roasting. If my buttocks became wheels and my spirits a horse, I would ride them—what need would I have for a wagon? For we were born because it was time, and we die in accordance with nature . . . That is the way it has always been. Why should I be upset?"

Making jokes about your physical challenges requires a deep-seated humor, and this type of bone-deep Taoist humor is

Slowing Down for a Laugh

Once or twice today, slow down in your own hurry to get all your Very Important Tasks accomplished. Spend half a minute in the hallway or in the grocery store to chat with an acquaintance. As the pleasantries develop, be alert to an opportunity for a joke, quip, or ironic comment. Look for the opportunity, and take it.

Then chuckle. Maybe even a full-blown laugh. *Let the warmth of the chuckle or laugh wash over you. Enjoy the tingle, the fresh air in your lungs and your head.*

not restricted to the times of *Chuang Tze.* Jill, our neighbor here in CoHousing, is a survivor of breast cancer. She presents comedy routines about the grueling process of dealing with cancer to audiences up and down the state, giving the gift of laughter to those who are struggling with the disease, as she did.

Even the dim-witted Confucius finally understands the Taoist approach, and summarizes it thusly, according to the *Chuang Tze:* "Live so that you are at ease, in harmony with the world, and full of joy. Day and night, share the springtime with all things." John Blofeld, 2,500 years later, noticed the same traits in Taoists: ". . . their ready smiles and laughter, their joy in things so simple that other people, unaware of the holiness of every leaf or puff of air, would have allowed them to pass unnoticed."

Day and night, share the springtime with all things. That is a Taoist practice that the modern West sorely needs.

We seem to be so bloody serious! The Tao is pulsing through the world, including us, the seasons turn in their majestic cycle, the moon rises and sets, rivers flow to the sea, babies are born and grow strong and sturdy, yet we rush around worrying about petty things all day, our brows wrinkled with grim determination, our mouths set in a hard frown.

Have you noticed the way many of us walk? A fast, scuttling pace, propelling ourselves grimly from one imagined crisis to the next. We drive the same way: fast, discourteous, quick to anger. Only the destination matters; the journey exists only to be accomplished as fast as possible, and heaven help anyone who slows us down or shows disrespect for the importance of our current crisis.

As John Blofeld's experiences and the selections from the *Chuang Tze* above illustrate, Taoists are always ready with a

Traffic Jokes

Next time someone cuts you off in traffic, let the urge to throttle them subside, and just observe how silly they look, darting in and out to get a precious ten or twenty seconds ahead in the race to the next exit or stoplight.

Let yourself laugh at their anxious hurry.

But be careful to give them room, so their silly rush doesn't lead to an accident.

quip, an ironic view, a joke—even if they're mortally ill. Perhaps nowhere in humans does the Tao flow as boisterously, as cleanly, as in laughter. Taoists are always laughing, often small private chuckles, but also big belly laughs, frequently in what others see as inappropriate circumstances.

Why all this laughter? Why do Taoists clown so much? Partly, I suppose, it's because we humans puff ourselves and our petty affairs up to such ludicrous heights. The huge gulf between our pompous self-concern and our actual modest place in the universe provokes humor. Confucius is the best example of this, and so he's cited often in the *Chuang Tze*. So that's part of it.

More fundamentally, however, Taoists are brimming with joy because they see a world in which the Tao is just positively bursting, flowing boisterously everywhere they look. What a kick! And because Taoists understand this flow and its basic rules, they seem to be lucky (or perhaps skillful) at aligning themselves with it, and partaking robustly in that glorious flow. And it is a kick. Sometimes "happy," sometimes "sad," but always rich and full of passion.

Never a dull moment, as my mom used to say so often.

So Taoists laugh. Joke. Clown around. **Nurturing the clown within** is a difficult Taoist habit for some modern Westerners. Some of us don't easily play the fool. But trust me. You'll get used to it. You can be a clown, because who gives a rip if you look silly? The Tao is flowing through you. You're

Clowning around in a monsoon on Mt. Emei

partaking in the fundamental ground of being. Enjoy, you clown. Make everything a game. Playact. Parody. Never to hurt someone, but always to provoke that precious laughter.

And remember what Tsu Yu and his broken body reminds us, that clowning around isn't restricted to your "good" days, when it's easy. In fact, keeping your robust good spirits is even more important—and enjoyable!—on your "bad" days. A.J.'s and Kyle and I were caught in a torrential monsoon downpour halfway up Emei Shan early one May. Totally unprepared, we were quickly drenched to the bone, and soon cold to boot. It didn't dampen A.J.'s and Kyle's ebullient good spirits a bit, though. The springtime in their hearts ran way deeper than a little rain and cold. Or a lot of rain and cold!

Clowns and Kids

Spend some time with the kids in your neighborhood. *Give them your full attention as you talk to them. Since they're not judgmental and not as bloody serious as we adults, you can gently tease them, or exaggerate shock or surprise at what they say.*

Practice your clown nature on them, at every opportunity.

Of course, we all have our own innate personalities. My Buddhist friend Jay is a quiet clown, ever ready with a teasing question, particularly for the many children in Valley Oaks Village. How many times I've seen mock surprise or shock or outrage light up his face as he kids with Ash and Lou and the other neighborhood kids. My buddy A.J., on the other hand, is a garrulous fellow who positively lights up any group he's in. A.J. glows as he regales his listeners with an endless flow of tales and miracles from his colorful life.

There are thousands of ways to be a clown. Discover yours.

Or become a real clown. Renee here at Valley Oaks Village retired and promptly went to clown school in San Francisco. She has several clown costumes, and a large collection of outrageous wigs and hats, which she regularly loans out to the children in the neighborhood. At our annual Valley Oaks Village talent shows, she can be relied upon to don her clown outfit and entertain. When she and her zany Polish boyfriend Zbig decided to marry, they held the ceremony in our Com-

Your Bag of Tricks

Begin a collection of crazy hats, like Renee. Or crazy ties. Put them in a box or bag. Bring out the collection at your next gathering of family or friends, and have each person choose one and wear it for the meal, or the evening.

Pretend that wearing these hats or ties is perfectly natural.

Remember that being a bit zany is okay.

Remember that life is a gift to be celebrated.

mon House. We sang "This little light of mine, I'm gonna let it shine," and they exchanged not rings but hats—big, crazy hats, of course. And they are very well married. Renee, by the way, is at the same time a clown and an articulate social activist. Hardly a week goes by without one of her letters to

How Many Taoists Does It Take to Screw in a Lightbulb?

When news spreads to the neighborhood kids that you're not a typical grim adult, you're likely to be bombarded with jokes by the kids. You'll quickly discover that kids have only a very weak grip on what makes a joke funny. Be prepared to hear a lot of very stupid jokes, jokes that, in fact, aren't a bit "funny."

Laugh, anyway.

the editor of the local paper, reminding all of us how important it is to work for peace and reconciliation.

As a side benefit to nurturing the clown within, we're all aware these days of the therapeutic aspects of humor and laughter. Ever since Norman Cousins rented all those Marx Brothers movies and laughed himself back to health, even dour physicians have caught on. When you laugh a lot, and all that Tao flows through you, your immune system just flat out works better. Everything works better.

Our family has a small core of cherished movies, movies that we own on video or, recently, DVD. We have a few adventure movies (*The Lord of the Rings, Star Wars, Harry Potter,* of course). But the very vast majority of our Barnett classics are comedies. Ash and Lou can quote line after line of Marx

---

Saying "Yes!"

This past weekend, Ash and a couple of friends threw together a girls' costume-and-pizza party. Strictly spur-of-the-moment. They spent the better part of an afternoon inventing colorful outfits, and wore them to the Common House to eat pizza together. (Tammy and I chipped in for the pizza. But we didn't hover around; this was the girls' party.)

Say "yes" today to a crazy, festive idea from a kid or friend.

Tomorrow, initiate one yourself.

Brothers movies, and several years ago acted out the mirror scene from *Duck Soup* in their school talent show. Danny Kaye is another favorite, especially his Walter Mitty movie and *The Court Jester*. We can't get too much Steve Martin, especially if he's partnered with Martin Short. Recently the kids have discovered the outrageous humor of Monty Python movies, and have taken to the time-honored practice of memorizing and quoting whole scenes of the nonsense. We probably have watched these various Barnett classics hundreds of times. You remember that I'm not fond of watching TV. Watching movies that make you laugh is okay, though, so long as it's done with a dose of moderation. The laughter trumps the electronic media, in this case.

Ash and Lou really, really enjoy making fun of their father. You have to understand that I'm pretty old-fashioned, and for the most part the kids are helpful and obedient in an old-fashioned way. With this background, it's okay to poke fun at Dad, because the respect and love are firmly established. So they do, and they relish it. Particular favorites are the time I "guaranteed" them they'd enjoy a Hawaiian music show coming through Chico, and it was so bad we walked out after ten minutes. They often repeat my solemn speech guaranteeing their enjoyment of it. Lou specializes in reenacting the time I tried to lift a chair at In-N-Out Burger to scoot it to a different table, only to discover the chair was permanently affixed to the floor. I've seen my futile attempt, and my flab-

Halloween Challenge

Okay, this is stretching things a bit, and it may be too much for you. But when Halloween next rolls around, consider dressing as a member of the opposite sex, and going to a party or strolling around downtown in your costume.

Several years ago, Tammy persuaded me to don a wig, rouge, and lipstick, and a tight dress with wads of Kleenex in strategic places. It was exhilarating.

Tammy hasn't let me do it since. She says I looked better in that dress than she ever did, and she didn't much like it.

bergasted response, probably a hundred times. It sends Ash into stitches every time Lou does it.

So I've discovered that if you're going to be a clown, to make fun of the world, then you'd better be ready to receive it as well as dish it out. It's all fair game, folks.

CHAPTER 10

The Myth of "Quality" Family Time

If you or some of your friends have families, you know how incredibly difficult it is to carve out time with the kids. Kids spend less time at home these days, don't they? Soccer, baseball, martial arts, choir, theater, music lessons, "young entrepreneur" camps—our modern world is full-to-bursting with "meaningful" activities for kids. Even when they're at home, the kids are drawn to the television, or the computer, or the VCR—"home entertainment" is an intimidating and readily available diversion that's nearly impossible to limit.

Hence our modern American invention of the concept of "quality" family time. If we can't spend much time with the kids, let's make sure that the little time we have is "quality." Can't argue with that, can you?

Sometimes I wonder about "quality time" and everything that's spawned it, though. Our Sacramento friends Steve and Kay have two boys, about the same ages as Ash and Lou. Until fairly recently, we'd spend the night at their place when we visited Sacramento, in the days when there was still room for four kids in the house. Steve's boys would stagger into the front room when they awoke in the morning, pajamas rumpled, eyes and muscles not yet warmed up and fully functioning. They'd get to Steve, reading the morning paper on their blue couch, and crawl onto his lap. He'd grunt a greeting, they'd growl in response, and so it would go for several minutes. They really woke up, finally, on their dad's lap every morning, as he more or less read the paper, sharing interesting stories or comics with them.

I don't believe I've ever seen more "quality" time between a parent and kids.

The claim that the Tao, a natural force pulsing through all animate and inanimate being, is the root of existence and the key to understanding how things work, has unsettling implications. The Tao flows everywhere. Nothing is or can be without it. The most refined aria in Puccini (*La Bohème*'s *"Che gelida manina,"* for my money) has no more Tao in it than the squawk of a scrawny chicken in a Kentucky barnyard.

This, of course, has rather surprising implications for everything we do, including family life. What this means is that changing your kids' diapers and wiping the snot off their runny noses is just as important and meaningful as taking them to Disneyland. *It means the height of quality time may be your kid staggering to your lap every morning and waking up there.* And, in fact, if a kid's visit to Disneyland is the one day a week (or month) that the kid spends with a divorced parent, then that time at Disneyland is even less valuable, because it's twisted with imbalanced expectations, with the unease of "getting to know someone," and ideals of "having a lot of fun."

Taoism is firmly focused on the real, which means recognizing the Tao in common things. Idealism is as foreign to Taoism as nihilism. Both idealism and nihilism reject the real, and replace it with substitutes that are, in fact, tepid, warped versions of the real. There's no more flow of the Tao in a visit to Disneyland than in a walk in the park, or snuggling in your mom's lap. Connecting with your kids forges the link between your ancestors who came before you, and all your descendants who'll come after you. Your kids are your link to eternity. **Being real with your kids, investing the time to become an integral part of their daily lives, is thus a Taoist practice.**

Some of my best time with Ash has been on the short walk from our front door to our car in the parking area. She often spontaneously put her hand in mine, back when she was six or seven. Sixty seconds hand in hand is real quality time. Several years ago, Lou and I were at the local Endangered Species Faire, where all sorts of education and conservation groups come together to strut their stuff and let kids have fun. There

Not Staying within the Lines

Best to face it straight on: if you're going to spend a lot of "real" time with your kids, you're going to be doing a lot of stupid and boring things.

Stupid and boring to you, that is. Great stuff, to your kids.

And I mean a lot. Seemingly endless games, like Shoots and Ladders, with no point to them. Scribbling madly with crayons, obliterating perfectly good drawings with no concept whatsoever of staying within the lines.

Just as you think your mind has irrevocably turned to mush, they'll ask you who Martin Luther King was, and why he got killed. That's when you know you're into the next phase.

Hang on. It's quite a ride.

was a juggler there, who Lou and I watched for a while. The juggler wandered off after he was through, leaving his pile of balls and rings and pins on the ground. (Chico is a trusting sort of a place, still.) Lou and I were a bit tuckered out after an hour wandering around, so we collapsed on the grass by the juggler's stuff. I reached over, picked up a ball, and rolled it to Lou. He stared at it for a moment, then hit it back. I stopped it, then put a spin on it as I sent it his way again. He squealed a bit as it curled by him, and spun it back to me. We repeated variations on this sequence for about ten minutes, not saying a

Respecting Your Kid's Talents

Within reason and the bounds of health and good taste, go where your kid leads.

Ash is crazy about acting and singing. We spend a lot of time taking her to play rehearsals. I've sat through more performances than I sometimes care to remember. But it's important to Ash, and she's learning things and having fun. So we support that. Surprisingly, I actually enjoy the plays often enough.

word other than the occasional squeals and soft laughs. I've never had any better quality time with Lou than that, sprawled on the grass, not saying a word.

Parents, do you want to be real with your kids, to connect with them in a way that the kids will respond to, and remember all their lives? Stay away from Disneyland. Instead, be there every morning when your kid wakes up, to a warm greeting from Mom or Dad. Tuck them in every night, with a hand on their shoulder and maybe even a good-night kiss. Repeat daily for as many years as you're privileged to have them with you. This is quality time. **Quality time is real time. And it's a function of the accumulated repetition of what we consider "small things" done over many months and years.**

The calculus is one of the great discoveries of humans. Calculus demonstrates that it is the cumulative effect of many small increments that come together to create reality. Even before Leibnitz and Newton discovered calculus in the West, Taoists in China realized that the "small" is chock-full of meaning, and that the "big" is often empty hype.

So I suspect that the modern American myth of "quality time" is an invention of parents who are too busy to spend time with their kids, reinforced by "professionals" who don't understand calculus or the Tao. In reality, there is no substitute for spending lots of time with your kids. None whatsoever. The hyped, special "quality" events of so-called "quality

Once a Parent, Always a Parent

Kids grown up and flown the coop? Maybe it wasn't as good as you wish it had been?

Hey, you're still a parent. *And you can still cultivate Taoist "real" quality time with your kids.*

Call them up on the phone every week or two. No special news to share, just to shoot the bull, see what's going on. Not a long call, but genuine.

Send them an interesting book or article once in a while. Stay away from books with a "message" that they might misinterpret. Maybe a rip-roaring adventure story, or a romance. Whatever, but something they'll enjoy.

If you're feeling brave, maybe send a photograph of the family when the kids were kids. Just a reminder that there were some really good times.

time" are special only in the sparse and imbalanced flow of Tao in their idealistic, setup situations. Conversely, no time with your kids is wasted, if you're real with them. In the Taoist view, wiping their noses, removing their poop from diapers, pulling them behind you in a wagon, exchanging inarticulate grunts with them on your lap, rolling a ball with them—all this is connecting. Big-time connecting.

This is the time to say it: watching TV with the kids generally doesn't count for "connection" time. Television in general is a wasteland, and encouraging TV-watching in your kids is right up there with providing limitless cotton candy to snack on, or free matches to experiment with. Not that it is corrosive altogether. Tammy and I would watch *Murder, She Wrote* with Heather and Holly for a few years, and it was fun trying to figure out "who done it." Good connection time,

Family Time

Have an electronic-free evening this weekend. Prepare beforehand with a list of family activities that don't involve TV, videos, or computers. Perhaps drawing, or painting around the kitchen table. Making up a story, each family member taking up where the previous one left off. (Make the end of your episode a real cliff-hanger!) Perhaps games, like Trivial Pursuit, or classics like Monopoly.

Halfway through, have a snack—popcorn, cheese and crackers, and a soda. Laugh a lot. Next week, add a night during the week. Or two.

arguing about clues and all. The girls could also watch a couple of hours of cartoons on Saturday mornings, while Dad made and served them waffles. But that was it, for TV. Poor Ash and Lou. They don't even get that!

So perhaps you and your kids can share an occasional TV show that's funny (in a positive way) or intriguing. But not much. There's not that much out there that's appropriate. And even if there were, TV just doesn't allow much connecting between you and your kids. Turn the damn thing off. Or at the very least put very severe and clear restrictions on the time the kids (and you!) can watch TV. And follow through.

What to do if you don't watch TV? Part of the freed-up time you can spend with your kids, remembering the Taoist view of quality time. Sit down and just shoot the bull with them. Learn what happened to them today. Ask them what the best part of their day was. What the worst part was. Listen to them. Don't preach or draw a lesson.

Carving out Connection Time

Go to your neighborhood bookstore, and locate the shelf of books on short, ten-minute activities to do with your kids. Distill a list of a dozen or two activities that seem most easily doable, and post it on the fridge. Get the necessary equipment.

Every day this week, carve out the time to do one short activity with your kid. (This is in addition to reading a book aloud with them just before bed, of course.)

Play catch with them if they're on a baseball team, no matter if you're lousy at playing catch and it hurts your back. Draw pictures with them. Ride bikes to the local convenience store and share a grape soda. Paint with them. Fold paper airplanes with them, and have games seeing whose can fly the farthest, or the highest. Our whole family spent several nights seeing who could fly a paper airplane up to the ceiling fan in our front room and land it there. Lou won, finally, after we'd all had a hell of a lot of fun. Lou's plane is still there, stuck into the light container below the blades of the fan.

Play cards with your kids, even their goofy games. For a while, Lou loved card games but couldn't get the hang of "rules." Every game of cards with Lou was a wild, lurching ride with the rules of the game changing with every discard, very often to Lou's advantage. Leave your attachment to order and

Got a Difficult Kid?

I've been there. Here's what helped me.

First, simplify your life and cultivate the Taoist habits.

*Then remember: **a difficult kid is a spiritual path,** an opportunity to learn and be challenged and reach deep. There's quality in the tough times, too.*

And then one day, they'll do something that makes you so proud you want to laugh and shout from the tallest building in town.

fairness behind when you play games with the kids, folks. It's the mutual activity that's important here, not strict adherence to those arbitrary rules. Although sooner or later they'll get old enough to play cards "adult" style, i.e., sticking to the rules.

Tammy and I had a weekly bridge session with Heather and Holly while they were in high school. Every Sunday afternoon (which often coincided with their just waking up after very late Saturday night festivities with their friends), we'd gather around a card table in the front room, put a Beatles album on, and play bridge. When I was the dummy (yes, even then it was a source of jokes), I'd go in the kitchen and brew some Chinese green tea, and we'd all play bridge and drink tea with the Beatles in the background. Talk about heaven.

Postscript

Okay, this is all very nice, but what if you haven't successfully nurtured and protected your relationship with your spouse, and gotten divorced after you've had kids? There it is. A big fat failure, but unfortunately real. Too broken to fix. What can you do to maintain the family, so important in the Taoist view, in a divorce? The failure of my marriage to Heather and Holly's mom, Donna, and its aftermath, taught me three things.

First, try to share the kids as equally as possible. Don't let Mommy become the parent and Daddy someone who visits every month (or vice versa). Kids need both a mom and a dad. Each provides something that the other isn't so good at.

Being Real, Being Physical

Being real with your kids means being physical with them, both Mom and Dad.

Having "good talks" is not all there is to connecting. The type of appropriate physical connecting changes as the kids grow up, of course.

Babies need to be held a lot. It's good for them, and good for you, too. Holding hands is a natural. Enjoy it as long as it's spontaneous.

Wrestling and roughhousing is big, at least for Dad. *Be playful and have fun, of course. Pull your punches and be sure you don't squash anyone. But wrestle with them. Most daughters will enjoy it as much as the sons. And when your daughter, and then later your son, outgrows wrestling with Dad, move on to the next stage.*

Put your hand on your adolescent's shoulder when you're talking to them sometimes. A playful nudge or punch is fun, so long as it's clearly lighthearted.

And hugs when the occasion is appropriate. This phase never ends.

Here in California, we call this coparenting. It is challenging, and the move from one household to the other household every week or so is a real hassle. Do it.

Second, especially now that you only have the kids half the time, make sure you connect with them while you've got them. Remember that the modern definition of "quality time" is dead wrong. Remember the calculus, and the Taoist realization that the small, common things are where the Tao flows most naturally and robustly. Spend time with the kids every morning and every evening, especially, when you have them. Unrushed, leisurely time.

Third, try very hard to be cordial with your "ex." I realize this is sometimes impossible. But remember, you've got kids to raise, still, and it's going to be a whole lot easier and more fulfilling for everyone if you work together on ground rules of conduct and expectations, and coordinate events and vacations. Donna and I met weekly while we were coparenting Heather and Holly, for four years. To our minds, this contributed to their growing into the happy, confident young women they became.

CHAPTER 11

Displaying the Sacred

What do you do the first time you enter the home of a friend? How do you "take in" the place? Your natural inclination is to take the measure of your friend by how they arrange what's in their home, right? When folks come into my home, they usually drift toward our half-wall bookshelf just off the living room, and spend a fair amount of time checking out what type of books are there, how they're arranged, whether they're dusty or well used. Me, I tend to look at the stuff on shelves and window ledges when I first go into a home. This "bric-a-brac" is a lot different for, say, an elderly lady (cute figurines of ballerinas and dogs) than for a young couple with babies (pacifiers and baby wipes). Tells you a lot about where their interests are and their energies are going, doesn't it?

I do the same "checking out" when I enter a restaurant, too. And like me, you've probably noticed that anywhere you go in the Chinese cultural world—not just in China, but Chinese restaurants in San Francisco and New York and Karachi and London—you see pretty much the same display in some corner, the little figure in ancient garb with a vase of plastic flowers and electric candles flanking him. He's usually one of the Eight Immortals of Taoist myth, or perhaps the Laughing Buddha. In traditional China, every home had a similar altar, in addition to the family altar. Even today, many homes still have these sacred corners in China.

The Chinese display these figures for purely practical reasons: the Ch'i concentrations associated with these patron saints exist still, and if you honor/revere/bribe the saints, their Ch'i will help you avert misfortune and gain advantage. These public and private displays also accomplish another benefit. They remind everyone of the culture's important figures. They embed everyday living in the richness of the shared experiences and wisdom of thousands of years.

We are not Chinese, most of us, in the West. **But we can remind ourselves of bedrock truths daily, by displaying our own collection of objects that speak to us of the Tao and its flow.** Displaying the sacred is a Taoist practice for the modern West.

Where to put your display? Someplace where you see it frequently in your daily routine. The very places that people check out when they enter your home. Hidden away in your spare bedroom won't work. We put ours smack in the middle of the living room, along a wall close to the front door. It's not large, occupying the top of a little three-shelf bookshelf, some four feet long by twelve inches. But it's clearly not a haphazard, top-of-counter arrangement of junk. Our friend Ellen gave us the altar cloth for the solstice last winter, a beautiful green piece with gold trim. We just drape it over the top of the bookcase, edges trailing over to each side. (The bookshelf itself is normal life, crammed with books and CDs and coloring books, all kid stuff.)

The objects on the altar shift and change through time, just as the Tao does. You can make the altar objects reflect the

A Place Where Life Is

Start living with the possibilities of where to locate your altar in your home or apartment. There's no hurry. Where do you like to "hang out" at home? Where do you spend time—your "living" space?

That's where your altar goes—a place that's visible and part of your everyday life. Don't worry about feng shui or good-fortune corners. Your altar belongs where it feels right to you, not someone else. Your altar spot won't be the same as your mom's or your best friend's. It's your spot, your altar, your life.

Once you find a good location, you'll need a flat surface. Your spot may already have a shelf or table there. Or you may want to put up a new shelf or even buy a new table. Whatever works for you.

season of the year. Or the season of your life. It's your altar. What's on it should speak to you, bring a smile to your face, reflect what connects you to the Tao these days. What's important in your life.

Ellen has two altar areas in her home. One is on a small table against the wall of her dining room, with a purple cloth of dancing female figures over it. Here she has a group of dried flowers and an earth goddess sculpture with ceremonial necklaces draped over it. Her second altar is defined by a strip of cloth on the tile counter bridging her kitchen and dining room. A wide bowl sits on one side, with many stones of interesting color or shape, as well as an oak gall, an acorn, and a seashell. On the other side, she has two candles in spiraling wooden holders, flanked by a rough stone and a sprig of dried stems capped with rows of purple flowers. Notice that these two altars are in the vicinity of her kitchen and dining room, the heart of her daily living space.

Our own altar in our front room is a bit different, as every altar should be. Currently, the left side has a fish painting done by daughter number two, Holly, as she was battling her cancer. The little jade owl that we inherited from Holly after her death sits beside the fish. In front of these are two glass frogs, green like Holly's owl, that Ash and Lou picked out from the gift shop of the Honolulu Academy of Arts last summer.

The center of the altar is dominated in back by an abstract painting done by Ashlyn last spring, full of movement and color. (We alternate this with a painting by Lou every few months.) In front of the painting is a gray stone in the shape of a miniature mountain, and three cone shells (the ones that have evolved poison darts to subdue their prey) with particularly intriguing patterns. The front center of the altar is a horizontal chime in a wood mounting, which makes a lovely sound when struck by its small wooden hammer. The right side has a photo of the family in back, in a goofy pose. Another stone of interesting texture sits in front of this, and a wooden necklace with a Honu sea turtle from Hawaii, that Ashlyn put on the altar a couple of weeks ago.

As you can see, the kids contribute to the altar on their own. The only stricture is that the place shouldn't be too crowded and junky. I am the enforcer of this rule, periodically removing objects when it gets too crowded. But this is a family altar, and everyone gets to contribute. Tammy, being attracted to Buddhism, even put a small Buddha on it several weeks ago, and that's fair. *Since this is a Taoist altar, nothing is forbidden, or too ordinary or small to go on the altar.* The Tao flows everywhere, remember. But it has to be stuff that means something to us, that reminds us of the flow of the Tao.

Just seeing the altar every time we enter the home, or as we're lounging or playing cards on the Chinese rug occupying the center of the living room, is a benefit. The altar is a constant visual reminder, and changes with the seasons and our experiences. But in addition, we have things to do at the altar. Anyone rings the chime whenever they feel like it. It's mainly me, but the kids occasionally do also. I feel that ring-

The Tao of Your Life

Nothing is forbidden on your altar. Does something remind you of the flow of the Tao? Then it's appropriate for your altar. Put it there, see how it "fits."

Mementos from special times and special people in your life are okay. *Old corsages; photos of family, friends, or special "guides"; Mom's favorite brooch; drawings; the stick shift from your first car; Dad's tie clip*

The Tao flows robustly in the natural world, of course. *Leaves, acorns, or stones from favorite walks or favorite places. Coral and seashells from your summer vacation. Feathers or skulls found in the wilderness.*

As your life changes, so will the objects on your altar. But keep it simple, uncluttered. You pay homage to the Tao *by your everyday "living" with the objects on your altar. You can also show respect by ringing a chime there, or lighting incense, or a candle. These gestures seem to activate the Ch'i in the objects, or maybe they just activate your appreciation of the altar. Try them out, and keep whatever speaks to you.*

ing the chime sort of activates all the good things about the altar. Beyond that, it simply has a lovely sound. I tried lighting incense at the altar for a while, but the incense bothers Tammy's nose, so that practice was discontinued. In its place, I got some of those small, short "tea candles." In front of Holly's fish painting I put a scallop shell, upended, into which a tea candle fits just perfectly. So I light a candle there every couple of days, usually in the evening, of course. I like the sight of the candlelight flickering off Holly's painting.

This is probably the place to admit that I like the ritual of ringing the chime and lighting the candles. Maybe you share this trait with me. Clearly, somewhere in our makeup there's a part of many of us that likes rituals. Candles and incense, bells and gongs and chimes—these are certainly a very common part of many cultures' religious expression. It sure speaks to me. I'm not even entirely sure why it speaks to me, but there it is.

So make your own altar. It probably won't be anything like ours or Ellen's, necessarily, although a Taoist altar would tend to have some objects from the natural world, I would think. Maybe also one of those small, tabletop water fountains you see everywhere these days. The *Tao Te Ching* tells us that "The highest good is like water. Water gives life to the ten thousand things and does not strive. It flows in places men reject, and so is like the Tao." Shinto altars in Japan very commonly have a citrus fruit (tangerine, usually), and a pile of salt. The salt is a purification element, reflecting the cleansing action of salt water. The tangerines represent good luck, an ancient Chinese symbol that John Nelson, author of *A Year in the Life of a Shinto Shrine,* thinks is due to their resemblance in shape and color to the sun, source of warmth and life.

Some altars can be spontaneous and short-lived. Several summers ago, our friends Jay and Penny and their son Tashi would join us frequently at Gator Junior, a favorite Barnett

Your Home as Celebration

Your altar is the special, defined space where you focus on the flow of the Tao. In a more general sense, you can begin to transform your entire home into a space that celebrates the flow of the Tao.

This weekend, begin looking *for art that "incarnates" the flow of the Tao for you, that "speaks" to you of life's vitality. This can include paintings, prints, sculpture, cloth hangings, fine China, vases, pitchers, jewelry—even your clothing. If you can afford expensive things, go for it. If not, get the cheaper renditions—that's okay. But obtain the art and bring it into your home and your life.*

Adorn your home and your body with beauty that celebrates the flow of the Tao.

Just remember: *the things themselves are not important; the flow of the Tao through them is the point. And the Tao flows in small and plain as much as big and fancy.*

Soon your home itself will be a celebration. Home indeed. Soon your life will be a celebration. Life indeed.

swimming hole in Upper Park. A huge rock shielded one corner of the creek from the main flow, so it was protected and shallow. We arranged midsized rocks around it to form a little wading pool for the kids, who were a bit small for the main creek. Jay told me how in Nepal, where he had spent time, folks would pile rocks to make small, stupalike mounds to mark sacred spots. So we marked our kids' wading spot with several such piles. It was fun, trying to find the right sequence of flat and slightly smaller rocks to create the highest mound. Dragonflies (flame skimmers, mainly, with the occasional blue-eyed darner) loved these mounds, alighting on them to rest while reconnoitering the territory before zooming off to snatch up more midair meals. We spent many happy summer hours, repairing our mounds and watching our kids and the dragonflies stumbling and darting (respectively) in the creek.

The winter rains came, particularly heavy that year, and, of course, the swollen, raging creek obliterated our mound-altars. Not just our mounds, but our wading pool, too. As well as the lovely, shaded, flat spot on the bank where we picnicked. All thoroughly demolished, by that water "that gives life to the ten

Boulders remain while shore and vegetation change.

thousand things, and does not strive." That's okay; the Tao flows, and change is constant. Only the huge defining rock remains, and I like to get myself and the kids up on it whenever we revisit Gator Junior, just to remind them that some things are relatively constant in the world, even in the middle of a creek.

When daughter number one, Heather, and I were traveling in Japan several winters ago, we went to Aoshima Island on the east coast of Kyushu. I wanted to see the strange "washboard" rocks on the shoreline, a peculiar geologic formation created by specific wave types hitting specific rock types there and off Taiwan's east coast, and nowhere else on the planet. Since this was a unique and special spot, Aoshima, of course, had a Shinto temple on the island. (I say "of course" because Shinto is similar to Taoism, sprung from the same North Asian shaman roots. Shinto reveres unusual features in the natural world, just as Taoism does.)

To indicate scale in the photo I was taking of a portion of the "washboard" formation, I laid my old pocketknife on the rock. This pocketknife was really special to me. The tip of the larger blade had been broken off in the Grand Canyon one midnight a decade earlier, as I desperately tried to repair some damage to our tent in a driving rainstorm. The knife was part of my history, my life. I took the photo of the washboard formation with the knife indicating scale, then Heather called out to show me something, and I walked away, leaving the knife.

That precious knife, as it turned out, was destined to be an offering on an impromptu washboard rock altar fronting the

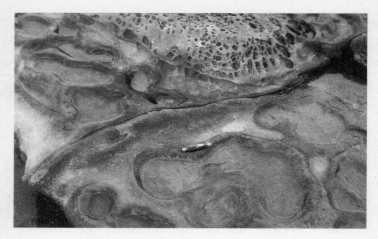

Offering to Ma Tze on Aoshima's washboard rocks

Aoshima Shinto shrine. The sea goddess, Ma Tze, she of the black visage staring out from bright silken vestments in shrines up and down the China coast, took the offering gratefully in the evening tide, and left me a mess of dried salt and some seaweed when I searched the site the next day, for my knife.

One of the most evocative altars I've heard of was seen by my friend John, now a professor of religious studies, when he traveled in Japan as a carefree youth. He had climbed to the top of a mountain, passed under the torii gateway indicating the presence of a sacred Shinto spot, and approached a rock column with only one object on it. The object was a clear, curved metal mirror, which simply reflected the enormous panoply of the sky above it, blue that day with dark clouds scudding across it. The sacred universe.

My Job Is Not My Life, But . . .

If you don't have something like your own "space" at work, then you won't have an altar there. That's okay.

But if you have your own office or cubicle or even just a desk, then an altar there is a possibility.

Your work altar won't be as personal and elaborate as the one at home. It can, in fact, be rather informal, and not even look like an "altar."

What reminds you of the flow of the Tao? That's what goes on your altar. It can be one or two things, modest and unobtrusive, and work well.

CHAPTER 12

Finish a Year, Start a Year

Does your past haunt you? It's a tricky business, dealing with the past. No doubt you've got your share of things you're not proud of from your past, if you're like me. On the other hand, you've probably got lots of sweet things from the past, too, that you'd like to hold on to. You know folks, I'm sure, whose past is the overriding determiner of their present and, likely, their future, folks for whom the legacy of the past is so overwhelming that it seems to have crushed the possibility of a new start, new life.

Not so in the Taoist tradition. The Tao is just as present and powerful right now as it was in the past. And the present is present but the past is past. That was then. This is now. The Tao can't be constrained or hampered. This Taoist emphasis on the eternal present is most evident in the traditional New Year's celebration in China and its neighbors. The New Year is emphatically a time when the past is put to rest, and the present and future joyfully greeted. This means all your obligations from the past year are fulfilled, your scores are settled, and your past year can be put to bed. The new year is greeted with all the fanfare and tricks imaginable to make it as prosperous and pleasant as possible, enlisting the potent aid of your ancestors and patron saints in this cause.

Of course, we celebrate New Year's in America, also, and doubtless you can remember your favorite New Year's party ever. Here, the family tends to break up into their separate, often alcohol-fueled parties. The Taoist-flavored New Year in China, though, is basically a family affair, with both public and family activities that last for a full two weeks. Putting the past behind you and ensuring prosperity in the future year is an important business, an enterprise that one night's raucous celebration simply can't accomplish.

It's probably not surprising that my favorite New Year's Eve occurred in Japan, when I was visiting my oldest daughter, Heather, there. It was dusk on this particular December 31, several years ago, at the Suwa Shinto shrine in Nagasaki. Savory, pungent smells wafted from the food stalls that lined the walkway winding up the hill through a dozen torii arches. It took us nearly an hour to get to the temple proper atop the hill, so dense was the crowd of people streaming to the temple. Also, I will admit, we did stop fairly frequently at those

That Was Then. This Is Now.

Sit down with a pen and paper and list the several things from your past that you're least proud of, things that you ought to have put behind you, but haven't.

Be brutally honest. Get them out. Don't dwell on them—this isn't about making you feel bad. But dredge them up, and put 'em on the list.

Okay. Fine. You weren't born to be a saint. You've screwed up. So what? It's the human condition. Resolve to learn from these mistakes.

Get some matches, some tongs if handy, and take your list to your back porch steps. Or some reasonably out-of-the-way place far from smoke alarms and flammable material.

Strike the match and put the flame to the list. *Burn these unfortunate events out of your life. You've learned from them, but now they're over.*

Accept that the past is past. It's gone.

Look up at the sky. Smell the air. You're in the present now. The Tao is flowing in you, and in your world. Strongly. Welcome.

Keep the Taoist habits, and every Lunar New Year from now on, let the last year go and welcome the present.

food stalls, as we ate our way up through octopus chunks in a fried dumpling with sweet sauce, roasted corn cobs, *mochi* with sweet bean paste inside, skewered cuttlefish, tempura vegeta-

Visitors to Suwa Shrine at New Year's

bles, sushi, sashimi, steaming tea, and more. Much of the time I frankly had no clear idea what it was that I was eating.

At the top of the hill, young *miko* attendants characteristic of Shinto shrines beamed in their bright red-and-white kimonos behind counters of magical talismans and amulets. Among these luck-conferring objects were wooden placards with yin-potent tigers etched into them, and gorgeous purple silk bags with white tassels, containing tiny, bright red scrolls of prayers for good fortune. The black-and-white *hamaya* arrows to frighten off misfortune were my favorites, although the biggest fright I received that evening was when the lovely *miko* girl told me how much my initial selection of amulets would cost.

Miko *attendants and amulets*

There were several thousand people in the open temple grounds by eleven P.M., and Heather and I had to struggle to get to the pond to see the brightly colored *koi* sparkle in the lights as they undulated through the water, throwing flashes of black, gold, and white. We all massed under the stars in front of the main altar as midnight approached, excitement and laughter bubbling through the crowd, everyone oblivious to the cold. At the booming of the drums marking the new year, a metal wave of coins arched from upthrust hands toward the front of the temple, where they showered onto the screening there and shimmered down into the collection box. Much yelling of *"O toshte omedeto!"* ("Congratulations! The year has turned!") shook the temple grounds. Never have I begun a year better. Or better fed.

Shinto is Japan's equivalent to Taoism, and the celebration Heather and I were part of that night in Nagasaki had many Taoist elements in it. Outside, under the stars, amid trees and fish ponds. Taking pleasure in food and bright colors and the prospect of good fortune. All keyed to a seasonal cycle.

Unlike the Japanese, most Chinese still celebrate the traditional Lunar New Year, falling on the first new moon between January 21 and February 19. The Lunar New Year is easily the most festive holiday in the Chinese calendar. Business and other matters are pressed to conclusion the last several weeks of the old lunar year. You must close off your affairs and greet the new year with a clean slate, both professionally and personally. **Putting the past behind us, and starting afresh every year, is a Taoist habit that would do us all good to observe.**

The Chinese have a rich collection of observances to embody this "putting the past to rest." A week before the new moon, the kitchen "god" ("saint" is more accurate) is sent to report to the Jade Emperor on the family's conduct. This is accomplished by taking the kitchen god's picture that has resided above the stove all year—this being the center of family activity—and ceremonially burning it, thus sending the saint up to Heaven with the smoke. His mouth is smeared with honey before he is sent, to ensure that he says only sweet words about the family to the Jade Emperor. Failing that, very glutinous—sticky—rice is ritually given to him, so that he'll only be able to mumble unintelligibly!

On the eve of the new near, the Chinese family gathers from its scattered locations; this is a family holiday. Wearing new clothes, often of the auspicious and celebratory red color, the children receive red envelopes of New Year's money from the adults, as they respectfully wish their elders a prosperous new year. The home is filled with new decorations: "spring couplets" of fine calligraphy on either side of doorways, the characters passing on ancient wise sayings; papercuts of door "gods" and folk heroes and heroines brightening the home with their intense colors as they protect the family; bowls of oranges and tangerines, symbolic of the sun which has been slowly giving more warmth and light since the winter solstice. The family eats an enormous dinner, consisting of many courses of the finest food. They show reverence to the family ancestors at the family altar. The night is spent in card games and other entertainments. The longer the children stay awake, the longer their parents will live. At midnight, with the new year's advent, firecrackers burst into the nighttime quiet, frightening off mischievous spirits who would dog your new year.

Public dances and other festivities are held in the two weeks after the new moon signaling the new year. The culmination of the two-week holiday is the Lantern Festival on the night of the new year's first full moon. Everyone strolls around outside in the light of the glowing moon, admiring the ingenious designs on the multitude of lanterns. Parades during the Lantern Festival often feature clowns, stilt-walkers, costumed figures of the Eight Immortals of Taoist lore, and culminate in lion and dragon dances. These dragon dances have become the defining event of the Lunar New Year celebration in San Francisco and other cities with large Chinese populations.

The lunar new year is thus a two-week celebration, stretching from the new moon to the full moon. The celebration begins as a family affair, then blossoms into a public festival. The past year is decisively cast off, and a fresh start is given to all. As with the Shinto celebrations in Japan, you notice many Taoist aspects in this celebration: the emphasis on family, the cyclical view of the year, the honoring of ancestors and patron saints, the enjoyment of the full moon, and the acceptance of the sacred in the everyday life of the new year (food, visits with friends, firecrackers, walks in the moonlight).

You will probably find it a challenge to incorporate something like this festival into our modern life in the West. Our own Gregorian calendar new year, with its emphasis on the family splitting up and going their own way to raucous parties, is hard to overcome. If you can forge a Taoist New Year's celebration on December 31, more power to you. We Barnetts stick together as a family on December 31, but we don't attempt to duplicate the Chinese lunar new year then. Instead, we celebrate two new years during the season. We have a family-oriented, progressive dinner party with our neigh-

Celebrate the Lunar New Year!

Get a Farmers' Almanac, *and pinpoint the new moon between January 21 and February 19.* Circle the date on your calendar.

Begin to acquire Chinese lunar new year posters and decorations over the next several months. Surf the Web for them. Visit your nearest Chinatown, and inquire. Check at stores selling supplies for teachers. Draw your own if you can't find any.

As the lunar new year approaches, take steps to put your affairs in order. *If you're on poor terms with someone, give them a call and make your best effort to straighten it out. Pay your debts. Terminate disputes that are dragging on, with a compromise solution. When the eve of the lunar new year arrives, put up your decorations and order a big platter of food from a good Chinese restaurant. (No, they're not all good.) Gather your family, and perhaps some friends.*

Remind your family and friends that it's traditional to put your affairs in order at the end of the year. Perhaps describe how you did it for yourself. Tell them that in the Taoist view, when you take these reasonable steps, then things from the past year belong to the past, which is given to the universe tonight. *Assure them that in the Taoist tradition, the past is past, and that tonight everyone starts with a clean slate.*

Then eat, drink, and be merry! It's a new year, a fresh start!

bors here at Valley Oaks Village on December 31. Even Lou managed to stay up until midnight this past New Year.

Then, a month or two later, we incorporate the Taoist viewpoint in our own family celebration of the lunar new year. Pinpointing the date of the lunar new year is the first step. Find a calendar (or the venerable *Farmers' Almanac*) with the new moons indicated on it: the lunar new year is the first new moon between January 21 and February 19. (Be careful about simply calling up the San Francisco Chinese Chamber of Commerce and asking them when their Dragon Dance Festival is held. This tourist-targeted festival is held on a convenient weekend somewhere (usually) between the new moon of the new year and the full moon of the Lantern Festival; you'll still have to get a calendar to let you know the actual date of the new moon.)

Once you know the date of the first new moon of the lunar year, then you can set the night before for your celebration. We actually start our lunar new year activities a week before, the traditional time for sending off the kitchen god. Heather comes up from her home in Sacramento, and we smear some honey on the mouth of the kitchen god's painting that has been on the wall above our stove for a year. We take him outside and gather around him while Dad grasps him with a pair of tongs. Then one of the kids puts the match to him, and up he goes in flames to report to the Jade Emperor. (This is done on the concrete front stoop, of course, not in a field of dry grass!)

We then immediately repair to the kitchen table and draw the next year's image of the kitchen god, as well as various other drawings to keep him company over the stove. Tammy is a watercolorist, so she and the kids do watercolors, while Heather and I stick with colored pencils. In the past, Tammy, as the best artist of the family, has done the kitchen god portrait, but last year Lou (who inherited his mom's talent) drew a wonderful, impressionistic, swirling kitchen god, which, we all agreed, would be the main image for the next year. The other drawings vary from year to year: a tiger, butterflies, a vase of cooking oil, matches to send the kitchen god up to the Jade Emperor, whatever strikes our fancy.

Even though the new kitchen god isn't supposed to be put above the hearth until the eve of the new year, we go ahead and pin him to the wall above the stove that same night, amid much ceremony, of course. It's always a pleasant, colorful wall to look at as we go about our kitchenly activities for the next year, between the kitchen god and his attendant images on either side.

About the same time, we put up colorful lanterns and festive wall hangings around the living room, traditional Chinese decorations that we've picked up over the years from school supply houses and Chinatown in San Francisco. The home really takes on a bright, celebratory look, which is much appreciated in the cold, short days of the end of winter. We also put up our Ancestor Table now, complete with photographs of those who have come before us, and are now gone. We gather informally around this table each night for the next week, reminiscing about the people depicted there, recounting their adventures, their hard times and their good times.

Then, on the actual eve before the new moon, we order a tray of appetizers from a local Chinese restaurant and nibble on them before pulling out the sleeping bags and yoga mats to all sleep together on the floor in the front room. Of course, the kids get to stay up as late as they want. Remember, late hours for the children mean long life for the parents! We spend the time playing cards and board games.

Just before bed, the whole family gathers around a bronze gong I bought in Korea many years ago. We each talk for a minute or two, in turn, about what the past year has been like, and what we want to concentrate on the next year. When each of us is through, he or she rings the gong. (If you don't have a gong, you can light candles.) These little reflections have been a highlight of our life as a family. They are moments when we can open ourselves up more than we usually do—even the kids—and talk about what is deep in our hearts. It is a rich, full few moments together, sometimes very happy, sometimes very sad, a time of tears as well as smiles. We all look forward to this time.

We avoid New Year's "resolutions." *Taoism is about what is modest and real.* Idealistic, hyped goals that require heroic efforts—and thus often fail—are not part of the Taoist life.

Then to bed together in the living room. In the morning the kids get small presents and we all wish each other happy new year and get on with our lives. We take the decorations down a week or so later. The old year has been acknowledged, its tough sides as well as its easy sides. The new year has been well welcomed and we're all fresh and eager to see what it brings, what new adventures will spring from the Tao. Happy New Year!

CHAPTER 13

Digging In

In China, the popular religion of Taoism is primarily a public phenomenon. The festivals and their attendant celebrations revolve around the village temples. The personal habits that reflect the Taoist outlook are too common, too deeply embedded into the fabric of life in China to warrant comment or notice there. They are, of course, nonetheless, a very real part of the Taoist living of life.

You'll have noticed that the Taoist habits we've discussed here have just the opposite emphasis, of course. They've been primarily at the personal and family levels. Since these habits are not an unconscious approach, embedded in our culture, we've had to hold them up and talk about them as Taoist habits. But we've so far pretty much ignored what the public, communal aspects of a Taoist way of living life in the modern West might be. That aspect is much more difficult to create, of course, than the personal and family aspects.

You can go a very long way incorporating the Taoist outlook into your own life by only taking up the personal and family habits that we've covered so far. These habits are, in fact, more vital and important than the public aspect. But these Taoist habits will take on added weight and richness if they are complemented by some community-level activities. A person or family adopting the habits is good; a group or community doing the habits together adds to the experience.

We should all "dig in" to the life of our local community, and become a part of the community's constant restructuring of itself. The community will not be an avowedly "Taoist" community, for most of us. Your own neighborhood or school or city is the focus here. And your contribution to that community's life will probably not be avowedly "Taoist," either. You'll be working for what is important to you, though, and those projects will be projects aligned with your Taoist values. The Tao doesn't require recognition. *The Tao doesn't need people talking about the Tao, or even knowing anything about "the Tao."* The Tao is perfectly content to just flow. Whatever you can do to help it flow smoothly and fully in the world and your fellow humans is to the good, whether you ever say the word "Tao" or not. So "digging in" doesn't mean proselytizing for Taoism—what an absurd idea! **"Digging in" simply**

means contributing to whatever helps the Tao flow more smoothly and robustly in your own community.

How do you do this? Simply bring aspects of your personal and family Taoist habits into the life of the community. All of us should be working for more public parks and natural spaces, for example. Places where everyone can be immersed in the Tao. Our neighborhoods and cities will benefit from it. The lives of our fellow citizens will benefit from it—not to mention our own lives. And these parks should have space where creeks can flow and trees can grow without human interference.

Four acres of concrete tennis courts do not constitute the kind of park we're talking about here. We need parks with room for trees to grow for centuries, for birds and insects and mammals to set up their homes and have a supply of food and burrows. A green, assiduously tended expanse of grass is better than concrete; but a natural area of trees and shrubs is much better yet. And if the trees and shrubs are native to your area, your park department won't have to apply water and pesticides to keep them healthy, and your local birds and mammals and insects will already be adapted to make a thriving living in them. And finally, if that natural area of native plants (attracting native animals) has a creek running through it, then you've got a little slice of heaven that will last forever with almost no upkeep. Treasure these areas!

Our Bidwell Park is such a blessed area, full of mainly na-

Greasing the Tao's Flow

Organize a park cleanup in your city. *Convince local firms to donate trash bags, a Dumpster, hauling to the landfill, and lunch for everyone. Make sure the event's well publicized.*

Then, when the day arrives, roll up your sleeves, put on your gloves, and start collecting all that trash!

And at the end of the day, step back and note how your park "breathes" better.

tive plants and animals. The park runs along either side of Chico Creek for eight miles as it spills down from the foothills of the Sierra Nevada. The "Upper Park" is undeveloped, consisting of a dirt road and trails. Joggers, bicyclers, and hikers use it a lot, as well as families that risk the rough road to drive in a ways and park next to favorite swimming holes along the creek. Along with the native trees and animals, it does have its share of common exotics, so it's not "pure." That's okay. Downstream from Upper Park, getting into the city proper, "Lower Park" has one complex with baseball fields and one large communal swimming hole, but for the most part it's also relatively natural, with picnic tables scattered in groves of majestic valley oaks up and down either side of the creek. Its asphalt roads along either side of the creek are heavily used by walkers, joggers, skaters, and bicyclers, and the picnic tables and little swimming holes are also well used.

Here in Chico we actually have sunrise services on the

Upper Bidwell Park—worth protecting!

summer solstice in Upper Park. I suspect that's unusual in most cities. Here in our CoHousing community of Valley Oaks Village, we have a winter solstice gathering, and summer solstice and equinox gatherings occasionally happen spontaneously, prompted by someone putting a note on the door to the Common House. These practices are also unusual in most neighborhoods, no doubt. But there's nothing preventing us all from putting together neighborhood or block parties celebrating the solstices or equinoxes. Put up some signs or call your friends, and gather to celebrate with food and drink and a good time.

The same goes for celebrating your "guides" to the good

Start Local

Don't know your neighbors as well as you'd like to? *Maybe you all drive straight to your homes, hit the garage-door opener, and disappear from view.*

Host a neighborhood get-together soon. Invite everyone on the block. Maybe on the birthday of one of your "guides." Maybe on a solstice or equinox. Maybe to celebrate the first nice weekend after a spell of rain. Maybe for no reason at all!

Please, no name tags. Just lots of food and drink, a potluck. You supply the beer and sodas. Be outside, if possible. Ping-Pong or croquet helps a lot, maybe badminton or volleyball. Let the Tao flow among you.

It's good to live in a community, isn't it?

life. We've had parties for Thomas Jefferson. Call a few friends together to celebrate the special days for some of your guides. We shouldn't ever be bashful about having parties! And so long as there's plenty of those old Chinese staples—food and drink—they'll always be a hit.

Participation in an avowedly Taoist gathering of people will not be possible for many of us, but some of us are fortunate enough to live in a city that has such a group meeting more or less regularly. If such is available, then "dig in" and become part of it, of course. All the Taoist habits will be enriched by such an association. If you don't have such a group currently, then consider forming one. If you can get one other person or family beyond yourself, then you're a group. You're not forming a church, remember. You're just an informal gathering of people who are interested in incorporating Taoist habits into their lives.

I recommend starting out very modestly in your Taoist gatherings. Enjoy each other's company. Talk about what is working and what isn't working for you. Practice some habits together, perhaps. Immerse yourselves in the Tao with hikes to local scenic spots. Get a guest speaker from the local college's religious studies department. Explore the Chinatown of a nearby large city. Have a group camping trip to the coast or a mountain. Whatever you do, don't be formal or stuffy. Your purpose is simply to share your living life along Taoist lines, in whatever way seems natural and spontaneous and enjoyable.

Part of a Taoist group's activities could, of course, be study of Taoist writings. You could read the *Tao Te Ching* or the *Chuang Tze* together and talk about it. Kristofer Schipper's *Taoist Body* is very good also. For a group of parents, William Martin's *Parent's Tao Te Ching* is wonderful. But I would strongly caution against merely having a "study group," without other activities. Remember the *Tao Te Ching*'s opening lines: "The Tao that can be told is not the eternal Tao. The name that can be named is not the eternal name." And other lines reinforce this point: "More words count less." "Those who know do not talk. Those who talk do not know."

Just sitting inside a room and reading a book and talking about it is not the vital center of a Taoist way. It's not even a

In the Trenches

Over the next several months, attend your local Park and Playground Commission meetings (or whatever it's called in your city/county).

Do your homework and research the issues, then speak up, from your Taoist perspective.

Advocate for the planting of more native trees and shrubs. The investigation of alternatives to chemical pesticides. Well-marked trails through natural areas. Places for folks to picnic and enjoy the outdoors.

If you're suited for it, and it won't throw your life out of kilter, consider running for a seat on the commission in the next election.

very important part of a Taoist way. The Taoist way is living life, not thinking about living life, or reading about living life, or talking about living life. Sure, we should read books about Taoism and should read the Taoist sourcebooks. But that's *preparatory* to living a Taoist life. That's a first step, which is useless unless it's followed by the vital next step: living the life that reading the book has helped you understand.

Perhaps the most important Taoist habit for us in modern America is this: put the book down, go outside, and live a Taoist life.

CHAPTER 14

But What About the Tough Cases?

You've no doubt noticed that the Taoist habits we've talked about pertain to the normal, everyday living of our lives. The habits that normal, decent folks can apply to their daily lives and see results.

All well and good. But we all occasionally bump up against a decidedly abnormal crisis, don't we? And we all, sooner or later, meet up with people that don't strike us as remotely normal or decent. Certainly we read about folks like this every day in the newspapers. What about serial murderers, rapists, and the perverts that prey on little kids? Surely these monsters aren't "already home" in the Taoist view? Surely the Tao doesn't flow in their horrible deeds? And what about good people who are struck with tragedy? Where's the sense in that?

These are tough cases. Can we make any sense of them, from a Taoist perspective?

Let's begin by reiterating that the flow of the Tao has nothing to do with human notions of right or wrong, good or evil. The Tao is not an entity that is loving or compassionate. The Tao is the pattern of existence, the inherent properties of matter and the flow of energy in the universe, "the mood of the universe." It is order and harmony, but it is not "good" or "compassionate." If you and I align ourselves with the Tao, we will tend to be more happy and perhaps more prosperous, but we won't necessarily be virtuous or loving. We will be centered, focused, at ease, sharing the springtime with all creatures. But we won't necessarily be model citizens displaying our society's notions of virtue. We follow the Tao, not American or Arab or Chinese notions of "good."

Having said that, we should also note that Taoists have long observed that when the Tao is present, the situation is characterized by harmony and prosperity. The Tao is supportive of life, and generates a harmonious pattern of existence. So how can the dark aspects of life occur? Let's consider a few of these aspects.

Violent Crimes, and War

The Taoist view of perpetrators of violent crimes is that they are creatures whose Ch'i has become horribly imbalanced. As we have said, humans are particularly sensitive creatures, with a heightened responsiveness to flows of Ch'i in their environment. In a typical environment, these Ch'i flows are not so strong that they nudge us far off balance. We all are somewhat off center, but not too much. The Taoist habits, routinely practiced, bring us back to center.

Some environments, though, are full of very strong Ch'i that pushes humans far off center. And some humans are incredibly sensitive to Ch'i from their environment, far more so than most of us. The combination of a person acutely sensitive to the Ch'i in their environment, and an environment that is full of strongly imbalanced Ch'i sources, can sometimes create what we call a monster. A person who is not "already home" or even close to it.

Hitler, a hypersensitive aspiring artist who (according to biographer Ian Kershaw, in *Hitler*) experienced the music of Wagner "as a religious experience, plunging him into deep and mystical fantasies," grew up under a smothering mother and a harsh father who beat him nearly every day. Hitler spent his early twenties in the Vienna of the crumbling Austro-Hungarian Empire, a city Kershaw describes as saturated with "the mood of disintegration and decay, anxiety and impotence, the sense that the old order was passing, the climate of a society in crisis." His rabid German nationalism at the start of World War I soon turned to the agonizing humiliation of defeat. In the bitter mood of Munich in the 1920s, the impressionable young man completed the forging of the future Nazi führer of the Third Reich, the decades of tumultuous

Ch'i currents producing a horribly imbalanced person who wrought destruction over an entire continent.

Monsters like Hitler and Stalin, and serial rapists and murderers, are far from the Tao. They have been pushed off center so far that their actions create dangerously imbalanced situations. Situations so imbalanced that some resolution, some discharge of the imbalance, is inevitable. And the resolution typically involves the release of a large amount of Ch'i—a destructive act.

In the Taoist view, then, people with massive Ch'i imbalances are quite literally "bent out of shape," out of human shape, at least. They are misaligned. Their acts of destruction depart from the Tao of humans. "If you delight in killing, you cannot fulfill yourself," according to the *Tao Te Ching.* Even killing for your country's defense or self-interest is no cause for rejoicing. "War should be conducted like a funeral," says the *Tao Te Ching.* "When many people are being killed, they should be mourned in heartfelt sorrow. That is why a victory must be observed like a funeral."

Taoists view war as a failure, an indication that the flow of the Tao has been ignored or abrogated. Some of my favorite lines from the *Tao Te Ching* express this: "When the Tao is present in the world, horses haul manure. When the Tao is absent from the world, warhorses are bred outside the city." In ancient, agricultural China, horses were properly used to recycle nutrients in agriculture. Breeding them for war, instead, was a departure from the Tao. Just as war itself is a departure from the Tao of humans.

This view of killing and violence as departures from the Tao, due to imbalanced Ch'i flow, has several ramifications. First, we humans have every right to guard ourselves from these violent expressions of imbalanced Ch'i. Just as prudent humans don't build their homes on flood plains and don't picnic on active volcanoes, so we do well to avoid those humans with imbalanced Ch'i. "Walk not in the company of evildoers," the Bible tells us. Stay away from the "bad" parts of town, our parents tell us. That's just Taoist common sense.

Beyond that, it's also Taoist common sense to avoid creating or sustaining situations where people are thrown seriously off balance. Neighborhoods where people are subjected to violence, and have no prospects for gainful employment, tend to warp some of the inhabitants and breed criminals. So it's in our self-interest to transform these neighborhoods, so that people can grow up safe, and live full, happy lives. "Social betterment" is far more effective than building more prisons, isn't it? Cheaper, too.

Granted, Taoists are not much into social betterment as a profession. But the point here is that the Taoist view of what produces warped humans leads to an understanding that better neighborhoods produce more balanced people in your society.

A second ramification of the Taoist view of horrible acts by humans is that these acts are not evil manifestations of

When I Walk on the Street Where You Live

Is there a "bad side" in your town? A part of town that seems threatening, a source of danger?

Remember that the Tao flows there.

Form or join a group of citizens exploring ways to improve the lot of those living there. Be real. *We're talking jobs, education, public safety, parks, and playgrounds—not just charity or sermons.*

powerful supernatural entities. In the Taoist view, there is no Satan, no Evil One that ensnares humans and sends us on diabolical missions with unnatural strength. Stories of incredibly powerful and evil wizards with a ring that enslaves the world are just that—stories. Good entertainment, granted, but not real.

What we humans label as "evil" is a departure from the normal harmonious flow of the Ch'i, but this departure is produced by the interplay of natural forces. That means that we can effectively respond to it. That means that we can take commonsense measures to reduce the "evil" in the world—measures such as social justice, jobs for folks, safe neighborhoods, the opportunity for a decent, productive life. "Sow justice, reap peace," as the saying goes.

You minimize the chances of Hitlers or serial rapists by simply producing a decent society where Taoist habits are embedded in the society. They don't need to be called "Taoist" habits. Nobody needs to perceive them as "Taoist" habits. But to the extent that your society is comprised of people who have access to experiences in the natural world, who are relaxed, who simplify their lives, who honor their ancestors, who celebrate their guides, who align themselves with the rhythms of the cosmos, who eat, sleep, and exercise appropriately, and who accept and accept and accept—to that extent, your society will produce healthy, happy people, and few monsters.

All very nice, you say. But what does a Taoist do with the monsters that we've already got?! Good question. First, you, of course, protect yourself and your family from them. That meant ostracism or banishment in the old days of wide-open spaces. Ship them off to Australia! Today, it may instead mean prison.

Prison. So, if you want to reduce the imbalance in a person, to restore the natural, harmonious flow of Ch'i in them, how should you structure the prison? Clearly, you will want to avoid sterile, man-made environments with no contact with the natural world. You'll also want to avoid passive, sedentary conditions where the Ch'i can't flow. Sitting in cells, spending a lot of time watching TV, in other words, would be the worst way to treat criminals. It can only accentuate the Ch'i imbalances.

From a Taoist perspective, modern American prisons are the worst way to deal with warped, imbalanced individuals. The Taoist perspective would urge us to get our incarcerated criminals outdoors. To give them meaningful physical tasks. To put them in some semblance of contact with "normal" life where the Ch'i is flowing robustly. From a Taoist perspective, repairing roads or reforesting burned areas or even producing gravel from stones is an improvement over today's prisons, assuming the physical, outdoor labor is supervised in a humanitarian manner. **The goal is to permit the Ch'i to begin flowing through prisoners, in a balanced way.**

Even better, of course, is teaching prisoners productive activities that they can use to make a decent living when they're released from prison. You get the Ch'i flowing in them while they're in prison, and give them a way to keep it flowing in appropriate balance when they walk outside the razor-wire fences and past the armed guards. The Sacramento County Sheriff's Department has partnered for a decade with Elk Grove Adult and Community Education to offer prisoners professional programs in landscaping, or business, or culinary arts. Vietnam immigrant Trung Van Bui has directed the Basic Food Preparation Program, as a way to repay America for the opportunities it has extended to him. What better way for Chef Bui to help America than by helping his inmate students regain their balance, and keep it?

If punishment is deemed appropriate for particularly violent crimes, then it's important to realize that you don't help society by locking people in cells for twenty years. This only makes them more imbalanced, more monstrous. We're only punishing ourselves when we do that, and raising the odds that these people will wreak more havoc when they are released back into society after having done their time.

Lubricating the Flow of the Tao

Do you have a skill or interest that you could impart to local prisoners? Some activity that would open up gainful employment for them, or open up the flow of the Tao in their lives?

Contact the sheriff or warden: is there a program you could plug into? If not, could a program be set up?

Try it out, and see how it feels to you.

The Taoist perspective suggests that if we desire to punish some criminals, then it's much better to have a swift, physical or social punishment, and let the debt be cleared. A Taoist approach would consider types of punishment that do not increase Ch'i imbalances, in place of confining people to steel cells for two or three decades.

Bad Things Happening to Good People

Another tough case is the good person that is struck down by tragedy. I have more experience with this than I would have chosen, having lost my twenty-three-year-old second daughter to cancer five years ago. Holly's death was a watershed in the life of our family. It was, of course, wrenching for her, and wrenching for us. Yet there it was—no escaping, no wriggling away from it. Holly had a lethal cancer that shrugged off all of modern medicine's efforts. She died four months after the diagnosis. We grieve for her still, and remember her every day.

We've come to two realizations from Holly's death. First, every person has a fate that may have nothing to do with how hard you work or how good you are. Taoists observing human lives for thousands of years have come to regard *fate* as real and inescapable. Mean, selfish individuals may prosper. Good-hearted, generous folks may suffer. That is fate. Do not expect to be "rewarded" for what your society regards as virtuous behavior. Do not even expect to be rewarded for following the Taoist habits. You are not in charge of your life, at the most fundamental level. *The Tao is in charge. And the Tao flows where the Tao flows.* It is grand, and not the least bit swayed by human wishes or desires. "Heaven and earth are ruthless," the *Tao Te Ching* tells us. "They regard the ten thousand creatures as straw."

Not being in charge of everything about our lives is hard for us modern Americans to accept. We demand perfection in our personal appearance and our behavior. We demand complete fairness in our society. Any departures from perfection and complete fairness are shocking, unnatural, "wrongs" to be righted, regardless of the personal or social cost.

The Taoist outlook is quite different. Humans are only a small part of any equation. The Tao has a flow and a rhythm that is far beyond human ability to control. **Fate is the acceptance of this modest view of humans and their influence on the universe, the understanding that humans**

Balancing Act

Do you spend more time and energy battling departures from your view of perfection than you do enjoying the vital flow of the Tao in the world?

More time in the office than outdoors?

More time objecting and criticizing than rejoicing and celebrating?

Take an afternoon off. Outline steps to put more balance in your life.

Then take those steps.

are set in a much larger perspective. Most people in the world understand fate far better than we Americans.

The second realization from Holly's death is that how long you live is not as important as how *well* you live. Many people approached me at the conclusion of the celebration ceremony for her life, with the remark that Holly seemed to pack many decades of life's experiences into her two decades of calendar life. In Taoist terms, the Tao flowed strongly and cleanly through Holly. Two decades of that is to be celebrated. We would all have liked for Holly to have had more than two decades, true. But Holly lived life deeply and richly. That makes her life a vibrant success. **From the perspective of the mighty Tao, flowing through eons and eons, the important thing for us humans is just to experience the**

Life Before Death

*If you knew you were going to die in a year,
 how would you live differently these next twelve months?*
*If you knew you were going to die in a month,
 how would you live differently these next 30 days?*
If you knew you were going to die,
 how would you live differently?

Tao fully. Whether it's for two decades or eight is less important.

I've mentioned Jack Paar's incisive observation that the important question is not whether there's life after death. The important question is whether there's life *before* death. For Holly, the answer was a resounding "Yes!" That's all that matters about any life, from a Taoist perspective.

Holly taught us—her family, her many friends—that lesson loud and clear. So we now do our best to live each day fully. We cleave to the Tao. We keep the Taoist habits that focus us and center us, so that our lives are rich and full. If we do these things, then death does not frighten us. "*Be always at one in the Tao, and accept whatever happens,*" Chuang Tze tells us in his writings. As Taoists, we do our level best to live so that it may be said of us, as Chuang Tze said of Lao Tze: "*He came because it was time. He left because he followed the natural flow. Be content with the moment . . . The wood is consumed, but the fire burns on, and we do not know when it will come to an end.*"

Epilogue
The Fruits of the Habits

All of our lives are suffused with our everyday habits. These habits contribute to a whole, an approach to life, whether consciously or not. And all of these habits have consequences, their fruits. That's the way life works.

What are the fruits of the Taoist habits outlined in this book?

Without doubt, the most important fruit is the deep-in-the-bones realization that you are, in fact, home. This world, and where you are in it, is exactly the place you are meant to be. Moreover, you accept that you are exactly the person you are meant to be, just as you are. You may have issues to work on, in the world or in yourself, but that's all right. The Tao flows, and transforms, and the same is true of you. Today, you are meant to be who you are, and you are home. And the same will be true for you tomorrow, wherever you are.

The Taoist habits reveal a world that is absolutely infused with the flow of the Tao, a wondrous and marvelous world. There certainly are dangers in the world, and heartache. Because you see the world as it really is, you may have some good fortune in avoiding the dangers and heartache. Or it may be your fate to live a life involving painful events. But just as you accept the sweet, so you accept the bitter. Both are involved in the flow of the Tao. It's exhilarating to participate in the world as it is, to know the mood of the universe with every fiber of your being.

The Taoist habits direct your energy to the real aspects of life. Your store of energy may be above normal or below normal, but none of it is wasted on fantasy views of reality. Fantasy views of how the world "should" be are high-maintenance systems. It takes a large amount of energy to cling to an idealistic (or a nihilistic) view of the world. The Taoist habits free you from wasting energy insisting that the world should be different from what it actually is. So you can devote all your energy to the real things of life. Savoring the sweetness of family and friends, the wildness and abundance of the natural world, the beauty of moonlit nights and sunlit mornings, the gifts of food and drink, and the pleasures of the body. Nothing detracts from these, not even the tragedies that may befall you, because all are part of the flow of the Tao.

The Taoist way is not to add and hoard. The Taoist way is

to subtract and let go, to simplify, to realize that the flow of the Tao is easily accessible. You leave behind the dissatisfaction with life that a single-minded striving for riches or strength implies. You realize that the key to life is acceptance and relaxation. That is how you ease yourself into the flow of the Tao. That flow may take you to riches and strength, perhaps, or it may not. Both are fine, if you get there by cleaving to the Tao, by being yourself.

So the fruit of the Taoist habits is just this: you dance through life, relaxed and utterly at home in a wondrous world. You dance, at one with the mood of the universe and its rhythms. In tune with the universe.

Cultivating the Habits

To aid you in cultivating these habits and making them part of your daily life, I include below a **summary list of the habits,** one that can be detached or photocopied and put on your dresser, or your refrigerator, or wherever you'll often see it. The habits are divided into those that are daily habits and those that are seasonable habits.

The *daily habits* will bring benefits to you according to the extent that you incorporate them into your daily living of life. Some of you may be ready to take up many of these habits immediately, and incorporate them smoothly into your lives. Others may not. I recommend a modest approach, in general. Rather than ambitiously trying to do everything, pick one habit that seems most accessible to you or to your family. Review the chapter that describes the habit. Concentrate on cultivating it for a week. Make it part of your everyday life. Your actual habit may be very similar to mine, described in the chapter, or it may be different, tailored to your own circumstances and your own family situation. That's fine.

If you feel you have made real progress after the week, then choose a second habit, and add that one to your daily living for a week. Maintain as much of the first habit in your life as you can, but concentrate on this next habit. Continue this through the list of the habits. When you have gone through the list once, start at the top and go through it again, incorporating the habits yet more deeply into the daily fabric of your personal and family life. Soon, most of the habits will be second nature, an effortless and smoothly integrated aspect of your life. You'll wonder how you ever lived any other way!

The *seasonal habits* occur periodically throughout the year. Sit down with a calendar with friends and family. Mark the dates that you'll be observing each seasonal habit. Anticipate the event. Make plans. Suspend your everyday chores and responsibilities during the celebration of these seasonal habits. Remember, these are holidays!

> "Live so that you are at ease,
>
> in harmony with the world, and full of joy.
>
> Day and night, share the springtime with all things . . ."
>
> —CONFUCIUS

Daily Habits

1. **Immersion in the Tao**—spend time in the natural world.
2. **Realizing you're already home**—relax, and simplify your life.
3. **Getting physical**—eat healthy, rest when you're tired, and exercise appropriately.
4. **Escaping the mental prison**—keep your mind and your worries in perspective.
5. **Accept, accept, accept**—let the Tao flow as it will; respect fate.
6. **The clown within you**—celebrate the Tao-drenched world.
7. **Quality family time**—it's the little things that count with your loved ones.
8. **Displaying the sacred**—make an altar to remind you what's important.
9. **Digging in**—work to help the Tao flow in your community.

Seasonal Habits

10. **Living in the seasons**—participate in the cosmic rhythms.
11. **Continuity with your ancestors**—show respect to those who came before.
12. **Celebrating your guides**—festive holidays to honor those who knew.
13. **Finishing a year, starting a year**—close the past and start anew, with gusto.

A NASCAR Driver Returns to His Roots

You don't have to give up your job and family and go live in the woods to rediscover your roots in the Tao. On the other hand, you can do just that. The following article on NASCAR Daytona 500 winner Ward Burton appeared in the *St. Petersburg Times* in July 2002.

FROM NATURE TO NASCAR

Ward Burton once lived in a mountain cabin without electricity or water. Now he's hearing a different roar.

by Mike Readling, *St. Petersburg Times*

WARD BURTON finished his second year at Elon College and still wasn't sure what he wanted to do with his life.

He knew he was good at philosophy and sociology but, as Burton learned, what you're good at and what you can make a living at are often two different things. Philosophy and sociology aren't typically high-paying career paths.

Business, his parents urged, go into business. There's stability and money in business, they said. Plus, the field is so expansive you're bound to find something you like in business school.

They had no idea how right they were.

Burton, driver of the No. 22 Dodge on the Winston Cup circuit, finally acceded to his parents' wishes and went back to the North Carolina college for one more semester of business classes. He found that what he liked had nothing to do with business. Or school, for that matter.

It was while he was earning sub-par grades in economics and business math that Burton decided it was time to do something he knew from years of hunting with his father and grandfather in his native Virginia. He went back to nature.

The next two and a half years changed his life.

"I didn't consciously do it, but after a month of kicking around, doing this and doing that, I decided I was going to go back to what I knew," Burton said. "And what I knew well and what I enjoyed was outdoors. I knew of a piece of land where there was a little cabin, and that's where I headed."

Burton, now 40, trekked to a 2,000-acre plot on the banks of the Banister River just north of his hometown of Danville, Va. The nearest community was 35 miles away. The nearest neighbor: 6 miles.

The plot included a cabin near the river and plenty of nature off which Burton could live.

He plucked catfish and bass from the river. He hunted and trapped for fur and meat. He raised a garden with fresh vegetables during the summer.

The 20-foot by 30-foot "four-stall tobacco barn" in which he resided had no electricity, no running water.

It was bare bones for Burton, who was 21 and 22 years old at the time. And it was exactly the way he liked it.

"I wasn't a hermit," Burton said. "I didn't have a family, so I was still dating at the time. During the week I was pretty busy."

"During the weekend, I would have some friends come over. But it was easy living that way. There's a lot of material things now that I certainly don't need. Nice house, swimming pool, things like that. I don't need all that junk to be happy. To be honest with you, the simpler you have your life, the easier it is to maintain and the easier it is to be happier as well."

His brother Jeff is six years younger and said he didn't

go to the cabin while Ward lived there. But the stories that came out of those woods are legendary.

"If it was a Saturday night, and you didn't have anything to do or anywhere to go, you could just head out to Ward's cabin," Jeff Burton said, referring to friends.

"There was always a party out there."

Not that Burton's life in the woods was all fun and games.

There was the constant upkeep of the cabin, its chimney and roof, not to mention the toting of fresh water for cooking and cleaning.

Then there was Burton's favorite thing: trapping.

During the winter, when the season was open, Burton would set out a couple hundred traps with the hopes of snaring beaver, otter, muskrat and raccoon. Checking those traps sometimes took more than six hours, starting before daybreak in the bitter cold. But the reward was well worth braving the elements.

"I made a good living off trapping," said Burton, who won the Daytona 500 in February but finished 41st in his last race, Sunday's Tropicana 400. "Back then, a beaver pelt was about $22 for a blanket, coon was $18, a good otter was anywhere from $20 to $30."

Eventually Burton found his way out of the woods. But when he returned to what many people would consider a normal life, working for his family's construction business, he was a changed man.

Little things didn't, and still don't, bother him. College and business school were no longer a concern. Life was different. Burton was different.

"I just kind of went back to my roots. After I came out of that, I felt a real peace of mind as well as some other things that being alone will make you bring out."

Upon his return to civilization, Burton often visited the South Boston (Va.) Speedway, his hometown track, to watch Jeff race on the weekends. One weekend Ward, who raced motocross bikes in college, found himself in a Volkswagen. The next week, he was driving a street stock and winning his first race in that class.

"I guess that's when the racing bug bit me a little bit," Burton said. "I had no focus, direction, or idea as to what the hell I was going to do, but I was (darned) sure gonna beat those guys in street stocks."

APPENDIX 2

The Traditional Chinese Solar Calendar

February	05	**Spring Begins**	*Li chun*
	19	The Rains	*Yu shui*
March	05	Insects Awaken	*Jing zhe*
	20	**Vernal Equinox**	*Chun fen*
April	05	Clear and Bright	*Ch'ing ming*
	20	Grain Rains	*Gu yu*
May	05	**Summer Begins**	*Li xia*
	21	Grain in Buds	*Xiao man*
June	06	Grain in Ear	*Mang zhong*
	21	**Summer Solstice**	*Xia zhu*
July	07	Small Heat	*Xiao shu*
	23	Great Heat	*Da shu*
August	07	**Autumn Begins**	*Li qiu*
	23	Heat Ebbs	*Chu shu*
September	08	White Dew	*Bai lu*
	23	**Autumnal Equinox**	*Qiu fen*
October	08	Cold Dew	*Han lu*
	23	Frost Descends	*Shuang jiang*
November	07	**Winter Begins**	*Li dong*
	22	Small Snow	*Xiao xue*
December	07	Great Snow	*Da xue*
	21	**Winter Solstice**	*Dong zhi*
January	06	Small Cold	*Xiao han*
	26	Great Cold	*Da han*

APPENDIX 3

Delving Deeper into Taoism

You've learned a lot about Taoism and the Taoist approach to life, just by reading about the Taoist habits that can be incorporated into your everyday living of life. Are you curious about Taoism? Want to learn more about it, and how it developed in China? Read on!

The most important thing for you to realize about Taoism in China is how complex it is, and how many different levels it encompasses. Just as in Christianity, there is a spectrum of practices and beliefs, ranging from the snake-handlers of Appalachia and the baptizing fire-and-brimstone "country preachers" of Texas, to the cool, vaulted cathedrals of Anglican England and the austere theology of Jesuits in Spain, so, too, the world of Taoism is vast. Indeed, due to its emerging

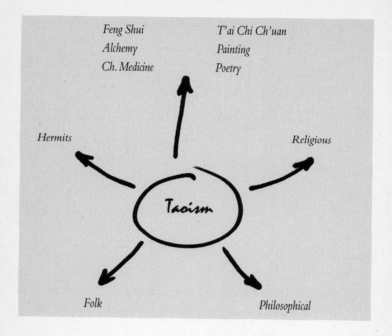

organically from several streams stretching back to the Paleolithic, and its lack of a historical founding event, Taoism's world is considerably broader and marked by more diverse strata even than Christianity.

Admitting that any catalog of Taoism's many levels is to a certain extent arbitrary, we can think of five reasonably distinct strata that stand out when one examines the bewildering variety of phenomena and practices associated with Taoism.

Lung Shan Temple, Taipei

Folk Taoism

Let's start with the most primitive and colorful of Taoism's levels, what I will term folk Taoism. This is the popular religion of China, the folk religion, and is centered in the temples you see scattered throughout the countryside, villages, and cities, even today. The temple activities are the modern manifestations of the Paleolithic shamans (*wu*), the magicians (*fangshi*), the local cults of river gods, and spirits of the sacred mountains where the totem ancestors of the families lived in the dawn of time. Through China's long existence as a culture and country, the local heroes and heroines of wars and

Ma Tze in the Tsu Hsien Temple, Taiwan

rebellions and local history were gradually added to these cults worshipped in the temples.

These temples provide the social glue holding the village and city neighborhood together. At these temples, in historical times, the various associations of the village met: the kung fu association, the lacquer and calligraphy groups, the various guilds of the city, the benevolence associations, the village elders. Even today, when you visit these temples as a tourist, you will see people bringing their children, their clothes, their cooking oil, their food, and even sometimes their new cars to be blessed by the lower-level "Redhead" shaman-priests of the temple.

You notice also that all ages and economic strata visit the temple daily to show their respect for the saints by lighting incense, bowing to the icons, and placing the burning incense in the urns fronting the altars. The icons in the altars are typically dressed in elaborate silk vestments, surrounded by magical mushrooms and clouds. You see many of the visitors drop to their knees before the icons and pray for good fortune for themselves and their families.

As you enter these temples in any village in China or Taiwan, what strikes you immediately is how different the atmosphere is from a Western church. There is not a shred of our Western hush and notion of "respect" inside a church. Here, you see children racing about being children. The "Redhead" shaman-priests smoke cigarettes between blessings. Men and women talk and laugh as they claim their blessed food and clothing from the table fronting the altar.

In a word, the temples are full of life, everyday boisterous life. Whatever else the practices of the temples are, they are definitely practices of life. The icons of the spirits are colorful, sometimes gaudy. Statues of tigers and leopards and fierce warriors crowd the altars. When I stand in these temples, whether in Taiwan, China, Honolulu, or San Francisco, I am reminded of a large family gathering, sometimes a circus, more than a Western church.

Temple life always features clouds of incense.

Chinese and Japanese scholars generally identify the popular religion of China as folk Taoism, as I do here. Western scholars of Taoism, however, are not sure what to make of this multifarious folk religion, and its relation to the Taoism of the Taoist priests. Is this folk religion a primitive form of Taoism, or a forerunner of Taoism? Or something different? The issue is very complex, and scholars are divided on how to formulate the relationship.

Viewed from outside the heady world of specialists,

though, it seems clear to me that Chinese folk religion is, in fact, simply folk Taoism, the less sophisticated forerunner of the "high Taoism" of the Taoist priests (*Tao shih*). These two levels of religious Taoism have a relationship very similar to that between Christianity's baptizing fire-and-brimstone revival meetings of rural Texas, and the elegant hymns and measured creeds of New England's Episcopalian churches.

Every historical figure you see represented by an icon on the altars of a temple began as a local cult in a village or region where the historical figure lived. Some of these cults, though, have grown to national, indeed international, prominence over thousands of years. Western scholars of China early referred to the icons in the temples as representing "gods," and remarked upon the astonishing number and variety of gods in Chinese folk religion. This misconception had its roots in our Western ideas of gods and divinities, and persists even today.

You should think of the figures of these cults not as "gods" or "spirits," but rather as "saints." These saints are conceived as representing constellations of Ch'i energy in that historical person so vibrant that, upon the person's death, the energy did not dissipate or come to rest in the ancestral energy constellation, but rather persisted on its own.

Worship by the people over the centuries reinforces and adds to the potency of this Ch'i energy nexus of the saint. Again, though, our Western term "worship" may not be an accurate description of what the common visitor to the temple is doing. The visitors you see presenting incense to the icon, and dropping to their knees before it, are showing respect, deference, and homage to the energy nexus of that figure. Clearly, they hope that some of that energy will rebound to them and bring good fortune to them and their family. Visitors to the icon may appear to you to be "worshipping a god"; but a more accurate and nuanced description would be that they are showing respect to a figure whose Ch'i energy nexus is so potent that it can hopefully be used to assure their own good fortune.

Philosophical Taoism

The next level of Taoism I'll introduce you to is quite different from folk Taoism. Very early in Chinese history, a more intellectual, distilled version of the strains present in folk Taoism emerged in artists, scholars, and leaders of the local communities. This phenomenon, which is generally called philosophical Taoism, left behind the shamanism and magical aspects of folk Taoism, and concentrated on the deeper philosophical foundations underlying folk Taoism. By the second century B.C., it had coalesced as the Huang-Lao School. Here, *Huang* (yellow) refers to the Yellow Emperor, mythological ruler in ancient China. *Lao* refers to Lao Tze (or Lao Chun), mythological (or perhaps historical) writer of the *Tao Te Ching*. The Huang–Lao School was originally a mystery religion, consisting of enlightened initiates who went beyond the superstitions and shamanism of folk Taoism. Their ideas were very much rooted in Lao Tze's classic and cryptic book, the *Tao Te Ching.*

While the Huang–Lao School has not survived as such, a persistent strata of artists and intellectuals in Chinese society has continued the practice of centering their lives on philosophical tenets expressed in the *Tao Te Ching,* and the later *Chuang Tze.* While folk Taoism recognizes the importance of these two sources, it overlays them with a vast assembage of other outlooks and practices. Philosophical Taoism, in whatever age, never strays far from these two written sources.

Philosophical Taoism has declined considerably in the past century in China, where the intellectual class has embraced Western ideas. When you travel in China, you find very few educated, English-speaking Chinese who want to talk about the Tao, or even have a very clear notion of what it is. Clearly, this level of philosophical Taoism is the most accessible to us Westerners, though, since it is not loaded with cults and rituals and all the other exotic practices of folk Taoism. It may not be preposterous to claim that you will find more philosophical Taoists in California and France today than in China!

Religious Taoism

Next is yet another level, termed religious Taoism, comprised by the body of professional Taoist priests, the Tao Shih. If the boisterous, colorful life of Chinese folk religion centered in the temples is folk Taoism, or "low Taoism," then the level of

Tao Shih constitutes "high Taoism," the official arm of religious Taoism. Tao Shih priests regard themselves as the unique and sole body entrusted with maintaining and passing on the orthodox understanding of official religious Taoism's vision of the nature of reality and the human place in reality.

Beyond this role of transmission, the Tao Shih cultivate in their own bodies the pure presence of the Tao, believing that they go beyond the mere human condition and become receptacles of the complete, undifferentiated flow of the Tao. By virtue of this, they are convinced they can balance ("rectify") perturbations in the flow of the Tao in their village, region, or nation. The phrase *Zhi shen, Zhi guo* expresses it: balance yourself, balance the empire. This ability to rectify the Ch'i is believed by Tao Shih to bring prosperity and ward off famine, war, bad governance, and similar misfortune on the regional and national level. On the local level, the Tao Shih's power is believed to cure disease and unfaithful spouses and bad luck in business, among other uses.

Whereas folk Taoism emerges out of ancient and various roots, the Tao Shih of official religious Taoism have a definite historical origin: the "New Covenant" (*Zhengyi*) received by the historical Chang Tao Ling in the second century A.D. in the Kingdom of Shu (today's Szechuan). Chang Tao Ling had a vision from Lao Chun, the spirit of Lao Tze. Lao Chun was concerned that the local cults and their shaman-priests were becoming corrupt and engaging in dangerous, misleading practices. He made a covenant with Chang Tao Ling to found a "new religion" that would supersede and combat this "old religion." The new religion was called Tian Shih, the Heavenly Masters' religion. Chang Tao Ling is the first Heavenly Master, in a hereditary line that stretches unbroken to this day. Today, the Tian Shih sect is officially labelled Zhengyi, the New Covenant.

Those to whom this new understanding is transmitted are the Tao Shih, the initiated Masters or priests of religious Taoism. *Tao Shih consider themselves the only true Taoists.* In their minds, the adjective "Taoist" can refer only to them and their practices. The "Redhead" shaman-priests of the temples, and the folk religion of the temple cults, is the "old religion" that the Tao Shih have gone beyond. Thus the Tao Shih visit the temples, and perform rituals of exorcism and rectification in the temples. But they are not officially associated with any given temple; they are associated only with the Tian Shih body of priests stretching down from Chang Tao Ling, or one of the newer reform sects.

The Tao Shih view the temple practices with the same unease and distaste that a Jesuit theologian would have for a Texas Baptist hellfire-and-brimstone revival meeting, or an Appalachian snake-handling session. The Tao Shih feel they are the containers and transmitters of the only true Taoism; they perform services for the folk at the temples, but they are independent of the temples and their superstitious cults.

If you want to see a Tao Shih, you'll have to go to a temple during one of the major festivals, when the local temple will hire the Tao Shih to conduct a ritual of cleansing or exorcism or blessing. You'll know the Tao Shih by his colorful robe and grave bearing, his expectation to be deferred to and fussed over. The Tao Shih contrasts strongly with the "Redhead" shaman-priest, whom you see daily at the temple, in strikingly informal garb and demeanor.

Over the two thousand years since Chang Tao Ling's new covenant with Lao Chun, a multitude of reform sects of religious Taoism have come into being in China, accommodating new understandings and new social aspects of Chinese civilization. Many of these new sects are reactions to the invasion of Buddhism into China from India. The Shangqing Taoist sect flourished on Mao Shan mountain south of Nanjing late in the fourth century, and emphasized meditation and the interiorization of the religious experience of its priests— both of these developments being Buddhist elements, of course. (This is the same Mao Shan referred to in the recent movie *Crouching Tiger, Hidden Dragon*.) The Lingbao Taoist sect a century later incorporated the Buddhist emphasis on elaborate ritual elements and personal salvation, again not emphasized in the original, Heavenly Masters, Taoism. The Zhuan Zhen Taoist sect was founded during the Mongol domination of China in the fourteenth century A.D. Again, new elements came from Buddhism, emphasizing monasteries of celibate monks devoted to perfecting the flow of the Tao in themselves through meditation and study.

Tao Shih of these and other sects received their training

within the schools of their own sect, but were all certified as Tao Shih by the reigning Heavenly Master of the Chang family line on Lunghu Shan (Dragon–Tiger Mountain) in Jiangxi province. Currently, the Taoist presence on Lunghu Shan is much reduced. The current Heavenly Master of the Chang family lives on Taiwan. Indeed, the number of Tao Shih in general has diminished drastically, particularly on mainland China.

Today, most Tao Shih belong to either the Zhengyi or Zhuan Zhen sect. Zhengyi priests are the modern presence of the Heavenly Masters tradition. They marry and have families and participate extensively in the life of the surrounding society. Zhuan Zhen priests are celibate and concentrate more on meditation and cultivation of the Tao. Regardless of the sect they formally identify with, all current Tao Shih draw upon the rich traditions of the entire development of Taoism in China, all the sects. It is probably safe to say, however, that the Zhengyi sect aligns itself more closely with the old, "orthodox" Heavenly Masters school of Taoism, predating the Buddhist influences so strong in the Zhuan Zhen sect.

Hermits

A fourth level of the Taoist world is that of recluses who renounce human society and live in the wilderness of mountains, perfecting their union with the Tao. A huge literature of wondrous tales of these eccentrics developed over the past several thousand years, with ample indulgence in the common human longing for the miraculous and for immortality. These marvelous personages care not a whit for rectifying Ch'i in society or blessing the clothes of children. They live in the pursuit (or enjoyment, perhaps) of complete Oneness with the Tao. Most are Tao Shih who leave families (if they are in the Heavenly Masters tradition) or monasteries (if from the Zhuan Zhen tradition) behind and take to the mountains. John Blofeld met many of these recluses in the 1930s, while wandering China. Although their number was reduced from the old days, these hermits were as eccentric and their company as intriguing as ever, as recounted in Blofeld's *Taoist Mysteries and Magic* (1973). Though they have not completely disappeared, Taoist hermits today are few in number.

Taoist-inspired Arts

The fifth and last level I will mention is the diverse collection of Taoist-inspired arts, movements in Chinese civilization that sprang from the vast "Taoist" assembly of levels and practices, without being formally linked to either low or high or philosophical Taoism. One example is the art of feng shui, being sensitive to "wind and water" in the placement of homes and buildings. Originally, feng shui was used to place tombs appropriately, so that residual Ch'i of the dead would rest comfortably. But soon it expanded with the realization that the living are also affected by the flow of Ch'i through the world.

Early-morning t'ai chi in a Beijing park

Another example is Chinese alchemy, the medieval investigation of properties of minerals and substances in China, and the rules of the transformation of substances. Many alchemists in China worked within a Taoist perspective, searching for the secret of immortality. As in the West, early science in China emerged from alchemical explorations. Another example is t'ai chi ch'uan, the "soft" martial art that emphasizes the constant transition from yin to yang to yin and the importance of smoothing the flow of Ch'i through the body.

No doubt you are thoroughly convinced by now that the phenomenon of "Taoism" in China is, indeed, vast and multifaceted. And no doubt you gather that when I have used the adjective "Taoist" in this book, I was referring in an informal way to any of the legion of perspectives and practices within the many levels that I have outlined above.

You recall that Tao Shih priests prefer to restrict the use of the term "Taoist" to only the "high Taoism" of the Tao Shih's religious Taoism. I respect their learning and their spiritual development, and understand their motivation for this wish. But it seems to me to be excessively proprietary. Taoism is a vast, messy, complex collection of many perspectives and practices. To my mind, no one level of this multifaceted phenomenon stretching over five thousand years of Chinese history can lay exclusive claim to the term. I use the term "Taoist," then, as an inclusive term, referring to the whole body of phenomenon I have outlined in this chapter.

You will notice that most of the habits I have emphasized in preceding chapters come from folk Taoism, and from the early Tian Shih (Zhengyi, "orthodox") school of religious Taoism. I do not claim that these two levels necessarily and in all cases adhere most closely to the distinctive Taoist outlook. I do feel, however, that folk Taoism and the Tian Shih tradition offer habits that are most useful and most easily incorporated into our modern American lives.